GREGORY MOTTON

TWO PLAYS

Ambulance

Downfall

OBERON BOOKS
LONDON

This collected edition first published by Oberon Books Ltd, 521
Caledonian Road, London N7 9RH

Tel: 0171 607 3637/Fax 0171 607 3629

Ambulance Copyright © Gregory Motton 1987

Downfall © Copyright Gregory Motton 1989

The Author has asserted his moral rights.

Gregory Motton is hereby identified as author of *Ambulance* and
Downfall in accordance with Section 77 of the Copyright, Designs
and Patents Act 1988.

ISBN 1 870259 61 0

Cover design: Andrzej Klimowski

Cover typography: Richard Doust

Printed in Great Britain by Rexam Digital Imaging Limited,
Reading.

CONTENTS

Ambulance

CHARACTERS

JOHNNY, forty

CLIVEY, twenty, black

MARTIN, thirty-seven

ELLIS, thirty eight, Martin's sister

PEDRO, thirty

TINA, twenty-three

LOUISE, twenty-seven

MARY, twenty-three, black

AMBULANCE CREW

*The action takes place on the street, outside a launderette
and also in Ellis's room*

Ambulance was first produced at the Royal Court Theatre in September 1987 with the following cast:

JOHNNY, Eamon Boland

CLIVEY, Robbie Gee

MARTIN, Adam Kotz

ELLIS, Patti Love

PEDRO, Kevin McMonagle

TINA, Wendy Nottingham

LOUISE, Julia Swift

MARY, Natasha Williams

DIRECTION: Lindsay Posner

DESIGN: Anabel Temple

MUSIC: Roland Perrin

ELLIS sitting on the pavement. Drinks down a pint of beer from a glass. Smashes the empty glass onto the pavement, gets up and walks off. Met by PEDRO who fails to get out of her way, they collide then stand staring at one another. Long pause.

PEDRO: Mind where you're going.

[*ELLIS mutters drunkenly, pushes past.*]

[*Stopping her.*] Tears. Don't just push past. What do you think I am? [*Seizes her by her filthy man's jacket.*] Having a drink were you? You broke the glass. I bet you're tough aren't you?

[*He boxes playfully with her. She stinks. She shies away in horror at being touched. PEDRO holds his arms out to embrace her. She looks up at him. Suddenly he points a finger at her threateningly and holds it there outstretched in front of him, then, just as suddenly, he releases it and his manner becomes friendly again.*]

Do you know what my wife told me once? The cosmos is chaos. You know what beauty is? Well there isn't any. You know what wisdom is? There isn't any. And form, there isn't any. Human ideas. Did you ever have an idea? About anything, the stars, for example. The Milky Way. That is an exaggeration. Look at it. I'm on the run, in a way, so are you. We've been too careless. But carelessness is an idea, an exaggeration.

What I'm trying to say to you is, don't cry. Don't worry, it's a kiss. Out of the blackness comes a kiss, and then all of a sudden, you bump your forehead on the moon's crusty surface. Born Again! Life is an extension of death, this is an extension of my arm!

[*He holds out his arm, moves closer to her with it, touches her ragged head. She remains still. He opens her shirt and puts his hand inside. She stands for a while as he caresses her, then pulls away in shame.*]

It's alright, I was at arm's length from the smell. What's wrong?

ELLIS: I can't forgive myself.

PEDRO: Whatever it is forget it.

ELLIS: I have. I don't have any pain.

PEDRO: That's because you're drunk.

ELLIS: No it isn't.

PEDRO: Well, we can't feel pain all the time, I wouldn't open my mouth. It's all there at the back of your throat, like tonsillitis, you feel it in the morning and then again at night, the day between is just an empty journey from one to the other.

ELLIS: [*Pulls him closer.*] I'll tell you what, you can forgive a person, anyone, even yourself, but to forgive the person you have to remember the crime. And I can't. I've forgotten what I did.

✳

[*Outside the launderette. MARTIN, a small withered man in his late thirties. Wears a blue nylon shirt open at the chest revealing twisted and burnt flesh, a red injury reaching to a disfigured ear and hair ill-growing at the side of his tiny skull. He walks stiffly and strangely with his head pulled back, his neck and chin taut. He clutches a white plastic bag to his stomach. His trousers are grey Terylene and stop short of his thin ankles. Short blue socks, moulded shoes. A small bandage around head and ear. He produces a broken pair of binoculars from his plastic bag and puts them to his eyes. Replaces them. Moves on. Stops.*

A lot of traffic. Lights and noise. MARTIN repeats his movement with binoculars. A girl, TINA, rushes out from the launderette carrying a bundle. She goes straight up to MARTIN.]

TINA: I've seen you before. This is my baby. I'm taking it somewhere where it's safe from those washing machines. The fumes are bad for him. Fumes like that can stop a baby breathing, destroy its intelligence, and all its physical reflexes. And the noise can give them a weak heart and make them cry all the time. What's the point of that eh? That's not much of a start in life is it? And it's not just the machines it's the people. They pull him and poke him; try to get his attention. They keep whispering things in his ear. They're trying to twist him, pull him out of shape before he's even human. They want to make him like them. I don't want him to die. I want him to live and be free. I'm going to put him here.

Don't tell anyone.

[She places the baby a little way off behind some cardboard boxes. MARTIN looks off into the darkness through the binoculars. After staring at her baby, TINA goes up to MARTIN.]

What are you looking for?

[MARTIN lowers his binoculars.]

✳

[CLIVEY stands alone on his crutches. He's nervous but trying to relax. Looks up at the sky. Pause. He hears a noise in some boxes behind him. Turns round with a start.]

✳

[*PEDRO is standing watching MARTIN.*]

PEDRO: Hey. Let me look through those.

[*MARTIN shies away.*]

Come on, I'll give them back. [*Comes up and takes the binoculars and looks through them.*] You can't see anything, it's black. No. It's orange. But you can't see anything. What are you looking for?

[*No reply.*]

I'll tell you what I'm looking for. An all-night chemist. My children are ill so I've got to get some medicine, quickly. All right. Do you know where one is?

[*MARTIN shakes his head.*]

The thing is, now I've got out of the house I can't bring myself to go back. Isn't that awful? My wife is nursing the children, they've got high temperatures. I don't feel too good myself. It's possible I may never go back. Or I may go back in a little while.

MARTIN: [*Puts his binoculars to his eyes again.*] I used to wear goggles when I swam under water.

PEDRO: Oh yeah? Where was that?

MARTIN: In the sea with the jellyfish.

PEDRO: Right. Good. And now you wear those right?

MARTIN: [*Looks at him and smiles.*] Yeah!

PEDRO: You look good in them. They go with your scar.

[*MARTIN turns away again.*]

I noticed it straight away. Disfigured, that's what you are mate. An industrial accident was it, or were you a baby and your mummy poured scalding water all over you?

[*Pause.*]

The world doesn't take care of its weaklings does it?

[*Gap. Music. They drink.*]

✳

[*Later. PEDRO is forcing MARTIN to drink from a beer can.*]

PEDRO: Go on drink it! That's it drink it all down! I want to see you swallow all this.

[*Shakes MARTIN.*] Drink!

Come here I want to hug you. [*Embraces MARTIN and hugs him hard to his own body.*] Your revolting body! It's like a fledgling's. Why didn't you grow? I bet your mother smoked.

[*Still hugging him he pulls down MARTIN's shirt and kisses his massive burn mark, following it down from his ear to his chest.*] Come on! Oo that's lovely.

[*PEDRO starts laughing and thrusting his hips towards MARTIN's groin until MARTIN falls over and PEDRO falls on top of him. Pause. PEDRO stands up and takes a few steps away not looking back at MARTIN.*]

How am I going to get out of here? Why did you bring me down a road that smells of fish? I could puke. It's everywhere. Look I've been down here a million times before. If I'd wanted to come down here again I would have asked you.

Come on get up.

Look at you, you're like a piece of string. My lips are probably infected. I'm not kissing *you* again. Would you like me to carry you? You look like you could do with a rest.

[*Approaches MARTIN, then pushes him away.*] Get out.
I'm not your bloody mother. You can crawl can't you?

Come on, I want to go now. Be quick. Right. Which
way? Right or left? Quickly! Left, OK. Hold my hand.
And if you run away I'll boot your ankles until they
bleed, OK? Martin, Martin you know what you're
looking for don't you? All-night chemist. You know
that don't you?

[*MARTIN stops walking.*]

Martin! Martin! [*Stops him.*] Smile!

[*They go off.*]

✳

[*LOUISE and CLIVEY.*]

CLIVEY: I was not with that girl!!

LOUISE: Oh leave me alone Clivey, I can't!

CLIVEY: Come on girl don't be stupid.

LOUISE: [*Seizes his crutch.*] If you say that again I'll brain
you with this, I will, I will!

CLIVEY: [*Hopping.*] Louise I can't stand up, come on
don't be silly.

[*LOUISE hits him with his crutch and he falls over.*]

Ow Louise my leg! Hey where are you going?! Listen
I've tried to be nice to you haven't I?

LOUISE: Get lost!

CLIVEY: You can't just leave me lying here on the
pavement like this! Ow it hurts!

LOUISE: Why not?

CLIVEY: At least help me get on a bus.

LOUISE: A bus!

CLIVEY: A bus. Just a bus!

LOUISE: Where are you going!?

CLIVEY: Nowhere.

LOUISE: You bastard!

CLIVEY: What's the matter with you?

LOUISE: You're going to her! Well you can. I'm going to have a drink, I'm going – [*Cries.*]

CLIVEY: Louise, it's all right. I won't get a bus. Let's go for a drink, both of us, come on.

LOUISE: No it's not all right! You're so selfish! Everybody says you are.

CLIVEY: Now you start laying into me about my personality. Why all the criticism eh? Is it because I can't stand up? It is isn't it? You'd like me to be always like this wouldn't you?

LOUISE: Listen, are you still my man?

CLIVEY: Come on Louise.

LOUISE: Are you my man?

CLIVEY: Yeah.

LOUISE: Then stop fucking that black whore!

✳

[*CLIVEY tries to move off, crawling. PEDRO catches sight of him.*]

PEDRO: Hey Martin, look. It's the Human Spider.

CLIVEY: Did you say to me man?

PEDRO: Hey it speaks.

CLIVEY: Do you want your face busted in half?

PEDRO: Watch it. Martin here has just finished telling me how he used to pull the legs off spiders when he was younger.

CLIVEY: You must be a very careless man to go around talking in that way. But I'm going to let you off if you put me on this bus that's coming along the road now.

PEDRO: You want me and Martin to put you on a bus?

CLIVEY: That's right.

PEDRO: You can't depend on Martin. His mother smoked too much. He sleeps with one eye open and his legs crossed. He can't lift anything, no flesh. You understand?

CLIVEY: You lift me.

PEDRO: All right. Martin, wave your withered limb at this bus. [*Lifts CLIVEY.*]

✳

[*TINA wanders about, seems to be looking for something without really looking. JOHNNY keeps his eye on her sensing that she will interfere with him.*]

JOHNNY: [*As TINA approaches.*] Go away.

TINA: What?

JOHNNY: Go away. I'm having a quiet drink by myself.

TINA: I -

JOHNNY: I'm a man, having a drink.

TINA: I'm looking for my baby.

JOHNNY: What are you asking me for? I can't give you a baby.

TINA: I can't find him anywhere.

JOHNNY: [*Seizing her by the scruff of the neck.*] Do I look like a man who's going to give you a baby from somewhere? I'm not going to give you anything. What are you going to give me?

TINA: Let go!

JOHNNY: Are you going to kiss a man like me? You're not going to bother me. [*Releases her.*]

[*TINA resumes her search instantly.*]

✳

[*MARY and CLIVEY in a room. She's kissing him and she's wrapping a bandage around his leg.*]

CLIVEY: Ow, mind my leg!

MARY: It's twisted around.

CLIVEY: What is?

MARY: This leg.

CLIVEY: I'll do it myself. Listen I've got to get some sleep...

MARY: You can't, the woman might come.

CLIVEY: So what?

MARY: What if she throws me out?

CLIVEY: You'll find somewhere else.

MARY: You said you'd find somewhere...

CLIVEY: Yeah well...

MARY: Come on let me finish your leg. The bandage is dangling.

CLIVEY: Let it dangle.

MARY: You don't care if I go back to prison.

CLIVEY: Come on, I hardly know you.

MARY: I know my legs are going to carry me back to prison. They stop all of a sudden as soon as I get out of a certain radius of Holloway...I've met so many people like you.

CLIVEY: Well luckily I've never met anyone quite like you before.

✳

[*TINA standing still, just about to move off. She sees MARTIN and PEDRO approaching.*]

TINA: Go away.

PEDRO: What?

TINA: Leave me alone.

PEDRO: We've only just got here.

[*TINA moves to go.*]

Are you going to be here long? [*Grabs her.*] Have you got a minute?

TINA: No.

PEDRO: Come on. Don't you want to strike it lucky? You might win something.

MARY: I don't want to win anything, let go.

PEDRO: There are prizes. [*Grabs her by the scruff of the neck.*] Look at me. There are prizes. Don't you want to win a prize?

TINA: No I don't.

PEDRO: I'm not dangerous, you're the dangerous one. Do we look dangerous? We're giving out the prizes.

TINA: [*Pleading.*] Please let go of me!

PEDRO: Look, don't get like that. You can have anything. Perfume, a box of tissues, just name it and we'll go and look for it.

Come on. You *do* want something. I can see it in your eyes. And you can see I want to give you something. Can't you? [*Lets go.*]

What's the matter with people these days? They're terrified.

[*TINA runs, bumps into MARTIN, runs off. LOUISE appears.*]

[*Spins round to LOUISE.*] Hey you!

✳

[*TINA standing alone. In the launderette, all the machines going. The swirling machines are giving out light like televisions. Their noise is music. Music that is washing machines and a clavichord waltz, it twinkles like the stars.*]

✳

[*Outside a launderette. Night. JOHNNY comes in with an armful of clothes followed by ELLIS, a woman with a boyish haircut and corduroy trousers with flared bottoms. She carries a plastic beer glass with a pint of beer in it, carefully trying to balance it so that it doesn't spill. She nevertheless is trying to pull JOHNNY back with her other hand.*]

ELLIS: Come on Johnny where are you going?

JOHNNY: Here. I told you. Leave off.

ELLIS: No but what for?

JOHNNY: Stop pulling my jumper you'll stretch it.

ELLIS: Come on Johnny.

JOHNNY: I'm going here all right?

ELLIS: Don't you love me any more Johnny? [*Tries to hug him.*]

JOHNNY: Put me down you've spilled my beer.

ELLIS: What's a bit of spilt beer...

JOHNNY: Bloody mess...

ELLIS: I've made the pavement dirty! Wait a minute I'll lick it up. Hold my beer please while I put my tongue on the floor.

JOHNNY: Don't be dirty, woman.

ELLIS: Come on Johnny, come down here with me and have a lick yourself.

JOHNNY: I want a young woman.

ELLIS: I am young. I'm twenty-six, thirty-six years old.

JOHNNY: You're too old, get up.

ELLIS: I'm twenty-six you bastard, come on.

JOHNNY: I need a young girl otherwise I'm useless.

ELLIS: What do you mean, isn't twenty-six young enough for you?

JOHNNY: Eighteen.

ELLIS: Oh you rotten bastard, you rotten bastard! [*Kicks at him from the ground.*]

JOHNNY: I don't like your wrinkles. You're wrinkled all over it makes me feel sick, come on get up.

ELLIS: Urgh I've wet myself!

JOHNNY: Oh you filthy cow get up!

ELLIS: Urggh! [*Cries.*]

JOHNNY: You piece of shite. Go away from me.

ELLIS: Help me!

JOHNNY: No, no step back, you'll make me smell.

ELLIS: It's all wet!

JOHNNY: [*Sniffs.*] It's beer you stupid bitch. You sat in your beer!

ELLIS: Oh! Oh! [*Shrieks with laughter.*] I sat in my beer! I thought I'd pissed myself. Whoo hoo!

JOHNNY: You're still wet anyway.

ELLIS: Are you thirsty?

[*JOHNNY hands her back the beer and turns to the door of the launderette which is closed. The lights are out except a night light.*]

JOHNNY: Open up!

ELLIS: I'm going to finish this off now so if you want a drink later you'll have to suck my trousers.

JOHNNY: What's the matter with them!

ELLIS: They're closed.

JOHNNY: Open this door!

ELLIS: They've gone to bed exhausted. It's all that scrubbing. It tires them out.

JOHNNY: They don't scrub, they have machines.

ELLIS: What?

JOHNNY: Machines. To do the washing.

ELLIS: Eh?

JOHNNY: Washing machines.

ELLIS: Bugger me.

JOHNNY: Obviously you've never been.

ELLIS: What? Here? I come here every day.

JOHNNY: You must have seen the machines then.

ELLIS: Of course I have. I just didn't know what they were for.

JOHNNY: What do you do here then?

ELLIS: Try on clothes.

JOHNNY: [*Rattles door.*] Open this launderette! I want to wash my clothes.

ELLIS: Don't worry about your clothes Johnny, nobody cares about that. It's the inner man...

JOHNNY: People want to see clean shirts.

[*JOHNNY starts thumping on the door. A voice from inside, 'All right, all right', the door is unlocked.*]

TINA: We're closed – *My Baby*!

[*TINA rushes out and seizes JOHNNY's bundle of clothes.*]

You've found him!

JOHNNY: No, no.

TINA: My baby!

JOHNNY: My clothes!

TINA: Give him to me!

JOHNNY: Stop pulling. This isn't your baby!

TINA: Let me see.

JOHNNY: Look, clothes see.

TINA: Where's my baby then?

JOHNNY: I don't know.

TINA: [*To ELLIS.*] Do you know this man took my baby from its pram, I was in a sweet shop. And now he won't give it back.

JOHNNY: These are just my clothes, I want to wash them.

TINA: And what about my baby's clothes, aren't you going to wash them?

JOHNNY: I haven't got your baby.

TINA: Yes you have.

JOHNNY: Will you wash these or not?

TINA: All right. Wait a minute. [*Turns to ELLIS.*] Have you seen my baby? This man is probably protecting someone, a young woman I reckon, just like me, but sad, you know what I mean? She must have been desperate. A bit mad. I forgive her but I want my baby back. Can you wait?

JOHNNY: What for?

TINA: They're so dirty. [*To ELLIS.*] Men are always full of dirt aren't they?

[*ELLIS steps back shyly. TINA is made suspicious. She points her finger from one to the other, her eyes ablaze.*]

You! You two are in it together. *You* stole my baby!

ELLIS: Leave off! I didn't steal your baby.

TINA: You did. You did! Why?! Oh please, please give him back to me. Please. You don't understand. He is mine. I'm his mother. You can't keep him.

ELLIS: Listen I haven't got him. I haven't even seen a baby for nineteen years so leave me alone.

JOHNNY: [*To TINA.*] Look you'd better go and put those in a machine or we'll be here all night.

TINA: I can't. I haven't got a basket.

JOHNNY: I'll get you one. [*Goes in.*]

[*TINA stands waiting holding the bundle of clothes to her breast.*]

ELLIS: Here, have some of this.

TINA: You don't know what it's like to be a mother. I look young to you don't I? I'm not really. I'm old. Older than you. This isn't my baby. This is a bundle of clothes.

[*JOHNNY comes with a basket. She dumps the bundle into the basket and goes.*]

ELLIS: [*Slumps against the wall, tired.*] Right. Where's she gone then?

JOHNNY: She's washing my clothes I hope.

ELLIS: She could have asked us in for a warm.

JOHNNY: A warm? It's not warm in there. It's the wind from those driers, they seem to get it from another universe.

ELLIS: I'm cold Johnny.

✱

[*PEDRO, MARTIN and LOUISE. Sitting.*]

PEDRO: Martin, this girl has lost her boyfriend.

LOUISE: Stop talking will ya.

PEDRO: Here, let me wipe all that make-up off your face.

LOUISE: Leave off!

PEDRO: I can't be your lover. I wish I could. I've got one. She's waiting for me. She's a mathematician.

I prefer friendship. I only wish Martin here was up to it. Listen, don't just sit there looking pissed off. Why don't you go home or something?

LOUISE: I'm not going back until he's there.

✳

[*JOHNNY and ELLIS still outside the launderette.*]

ELLIS: You know if you were to let me come home with you I'd make you a good home for you to be comfortable in...

You're such a fine man with your intelligence and your ... and what with me with my, with my...with my being a woman. We'd have a lovely time Johnny.

JOHNNY: Please don't, you'll stir painful memories.

ELLIS: What painful memories?

JOHNNY: I recall...I was sitting upstairs, the newspaper spread across my knees at the top of the house, and from down below where we had the bathroom I heard the sounds of my wife and my small daughter bathing together. The noise of the gentle splashing drifted up to me in my solitude and my daughter laughing and laughing and laughing until she sounded as if she was in pain, and her little voice, 'Mamma, mamma, mamma.' [*Pause.*] And now they are both gone.

ELLIS: Johnny you're lying. You were never married. You have no daughter!

JOHNNY: [*Sighs.*] Yes you're right. But does that make the pain of separation any easier to bear?

ELLIS: The fact is you are afraid of women. I think you are a bit scared of the meaty side of it, if you see what I mean. Women as you probably know are not like men, they are meatier. And I think it's that that bothers you. We -

JOHNNY: Please -

ELLIS: No I think I know what it is. It's because we're a bit like that meat you see hanging up in the butcher's, because you can stick your hand up inside of us and ruck it around and I suppose it feels a bit like when you're wrestling with that joint to get it into the oven.

JOHNNY: I wouldn't know.

✳

[*A clavichord waltz. Music that twinkles like the stars.*]

PEDRO: [*Shaking his head as if to clear it.*] Listen to that. I can't hear anything. Do you know I knew someone who used to clean out my ears for me.

Look I'm going deaf. It sounds like winter but it looks like summer.

I'm going to have to leave you soon. Martin and I have got an appointment. There's this midget you see who promised Martin to tell him his fortune. Only he's in prison. So we're going to wait outside the wall.

You can't come. You live around here don't you? So you can't. This is a mystery. We don't want the local residents interfering.

[*LOUISE drinks.*]

Stop that! Just for a moment can't you! Always the same bloody thing. Haven't you got any curiosity? I suppose you're going to sleep with your face in a bucket. You probably haven't even got a fortune. That's it. No wonder you're not interested. You stay here, we'll go on alone.

[*LOUISE struggles to her feet and moves off in the other direction.*]

[*Goes after her.*] Come on, you're not off to lover boy are you?

[*LOUISE keeps going.*]

He's too good for you! Come back!

There goes another one. The girls around here are like falling stars.

✳

[*ELLIS and JOHNNY outside the launderette.*]

ELLIS: So...I may be dirty and smelly on the outside, but once you get inside, I promise you I'm fresh as a baby.

JOHNNY: Look stop this!

✳

[*The time is broken by slow music. PEDRO and MARTIN standing apart.*]

PEDRO: [*Flicks up his eyes to the firmament.*] Look out Martin, look out!

[*Flicks up his eyes again and smiles.*]

✳

[*ELLIS and JOHNNY outside the launderette.*]

JOHNNY: Anyway, I'm not as inexperienced as you think, in fact I'm having an affair, with her.

ELLIS: Who?

JOHNNY: That girl in there.

ELLIS: What? Her?

JOHNNY: You heard what she said.

ELLIS: What?

JOHNNY: She said I'd taken her baby. Well I have. It's our baby. I'm the father. I've taken it away because I don't think she's fit to look after it properly. No, no you see, she couldn't educate it with books like I could.

ELLIS: Where is it then?

JOHNNY: Where is it?

ELLIS: Yeah where is it?

JOHNNY: At home.

ELLIS: What, on its own?

JOHNNY: No, no. The ambulance came and took it away. It wasn't well.

ELLIS: Oh.

JOHNNY: Yes they said she'd beaten it and they'd bring it back to me when it was better.

ELLIS: It's your child.

JOHNNY: Yes.

ELLIS: How?

JOHNNY: Eh?

ELLIS: How come?

JOHNNY: I kept coming here. Lots of things go on in here you know. Dances, parties. At night when you are out wandering around too drunk to notice.

ELLIS: No it's not true!

JOHNNY: Oh yes. Oh I've had some good times here. Lots of pretty girls used to come, and all sorts of people. Anyway she and I got acquainted.

ELLIS: [*Angry.*] What do you mean acquainted?

JOHNNY: Yes, she thought I was interesting. Interesting and handsome. Well anyway you know what it's like at parties, lots of kissing and that kind of thing.

ELLIS: Did she kiss *you*?

JOHNNY: Oh yes, not just me. But mostly me.

ELLIS: Ha, that doesn't make babies you know!

JOHNNY: No. We did it.

ELLIS: Where?

JOHNNY: Behind the washing machines.

ELLIS: You filthy bastard. It's not true, you're not capable.

JOHNNY: It's true! And actually it's one reason why I can't allow you to come home with me.

ELLIS: What do you mean?

JOHNNY: I have to create the right sort of moral environment for the child.

ELLIS: I'm not moral enough am I?

JOHNNY: It's not that. It's just that the young mind is impressionable. I don't want it to think I run around with lots of different women...

✳

[*MARTIN and PEDRO. A puff of smoke suddenly goes up from behind. PEDRO starts. Puts his arms around MARTIN to protect him.*]

MARTIN: What was that?

PEDRO: Don't worry Martin. It was just a puff of smoke from behind that petrol station. Look, it's all gone now. It wasn't anything, just some old boxes going up, that's all. Just a false wind. Just a false wind. It's gone now.

✳

[*Outside the launderette. ELLIS has her head in her hands.*]

ELLIS: I've got to have a piss. Where can I go? My legs won't carry me. Why's that eh? You tell me Johnny if you're so clever.

JOHNNY: I'll help you, come on.

ELLIS: No it's all right I can crawl.

[*LOUISE comes in. ELLIS arrives at LOUISE's feet.*]

Oh God.

[*ELLIS gets up stumbles over to some cardboard boxes behind. LOUISE stares at her. JOHNNY goes to LOUISE.*]

LOUISE: I'm sick of it Johnny, I'm sick of it.

JOHNNY: Are you? Come and have a few laughs with me.

LOUISE: He doesn't care.

JOHNNY: Doesn't he? That's terrible.

ELLIS: There's a baby behind here.

LOUISE: Do you know how he got his leg busted?

JOHNNY: No, no I don't.

LOUISE: Neither does he. He just woke up like it one morning.

ELLIS: [*From behind.*] It's wrapped up in a paper bag.

LOUISE: What if it spreads to the rest of his body? I might have to nurse him until he dies a twisted death.

JOHNNY: Ellis has been making up stories about me. She's accusing me of having sex in a launderette. She said there were wild parties there.

LOUISE: Did she?

JOHNNY: In here she means, right here. But really all I ever do is get my clothes washed. That's what I'm doing now.

LOUISE: [*Drinks, pause.*] Where's Ellis?

JOHNNY: She ran off.

✳

[*ELLIS's room where MARY and CLIVEY are asleep. Electric music, orangey lights from outside and a chip shop sign flashes on and off occasionally. A radio is playing in another part of the building. The window is open. Traffic noises filter up from the street. Below a man is singing 'When you're in love' over and over again.*]

[*ELLIS stumbles into the room carrying a bundle that is a baby.*]

ELLIS: Yes we're going home now. We're home. Isn't that nice eh? After all this time.

We'll warm you up in here. Nice and gently. I won't ask where you've been all this time because I don't want you to shock me.

But you mustn't ask me where I've been. I haven't been anywhere. No, I promise you. Nowhere at all in all these years. I haven't taken three steps in one direction or the other. I couldn't, in case you came back. I had to stay here. And I haven't done anything, I've just been passing the time.

But it's all over now.

We'll have a new beginning won't we love? Together.

[*Rocks the baby to her chest.*]

What's that bloody racket?

[*Runs to the window.*]

What's that bloody racket!

['*When you're in love*']

How can a baby sleep? Quiet down there!

[*CLIVEY rolls over in his sleep.*]

I'd put you in bed but that girl is there. I'll turn her out don't worry. I won't let her near you. She'll want you all for herself.

[*The music from the radio in another part of the building begins to get louder.*]

I knew this was going to happen. Do you know what happened the other day? I was looking for something amongst some cardboard boxes someone had left on the pavement and suddenly this dwarf jumped up out of all the rubbish and ran off down the road. He had tiny fat legs and an enormous fat head. He looked like a baby, he'd been asleep. I thought it was you.

I thought it was you my little sweetheart.

How can I get out of here?

You see, I keep thinking of all the damage you do to your children. You know, I would have done more harm to you if I hadn't deserted you. I'm such a terrible one. *He* was always telling me that. He was right.

Look at the place. I'm so untidy, I can never remember anything, and I eat rubbish. And I've got such a fierce temper. How I would have shouted at you. My eyes are rat's eyes. Rat's eyes.

Look at the way I'm holding you now. All tight and cruel. Fingers like traps.

I'd better put you down, right now. Yes, right now. [*Puts him down.*]

You would have been horrified if you'd seen me like I am now. It's horrible. Would you like to see?

[*Stands in front of a mirror.*]

My eyes are rats and they nibble at you while you are asleep.

He always said that. But it's not his fault. He was on the run; when we had − we did it by the seaside, on a stone.

My legs felt like rock afterwards.

He was, he was...oh he was hardly alive he was so scared of being caught and taken back. He said he was trying to stay alive long enough to make it across the Channel in one of those boats.

'Wait for my night to come,' he said. 'Wait for my night to come.' I don't know what he meant. Then he squeezed my breasts, he squeezed too hard and it hurt because he was a desperate boy he was. 'Watch the stars,' he said. 'Hold on and watch the stars.' And the stars jiggered about and I watched. His skin was black and his eyes were as big and brown as these. [*Fingers her nipples and then holds her sagging breasts.*]

Now look at them! They were volcanoes, now they've blown up and fallen down and everything else fell down with them!

Look at them!

All that melted mud on my belly in a sack. All the dead bodies.

[*Tears.*] 'You're going to see the world,' I said. 'I'd rather see your body,' he said.

[*She drops her trousers quickly and desperately. She wears a dirty pair of men's underpants.*]

Look, look all the walls have caved in. My belly button's gone as well. The world went down the plughole and filled it in. [*In tears.*] The world's gone down the bloody plughole!

[*She remains standing in front of the mirror. MARY has woken up and walked across the floor to ELLIS. Her young body is in contrast to ELLIS's worn-out one.*]

MARY: [*Gently.*] What's wrong woman?

[*The two women stand facing each other.*]

ELLIS: You step back in time and you find your whole life has been a nightmare.

MARY: What's that on the floor?

ELLIS: A baby.

MARY: Where did you get it?

ELLIS: I lost it and then I found it.

MARY: Where?

ELLIS: It's funny, I don't remember leaving it there.

[*CLIVEY, awake, comes over.*]

CLIVEY: What's going on?

[*ELLIS, shamed, pulls her clothes on awkwardly.*]

MARY: She's stolen a baby.

ELLIS: I did not steal it, it's mine. [*Gently.*] Who is he?

MARY: A friend of mine. How did you lose it?

ELLIS: [*Looks at CLIVEY.*] It's not my fault. I was very young. No one helped me. I just put it down and when I turned around it was gone. I never thought he would turn up. It's funny how things turn out isn't it?

CLIVEY: This must have been some time ago, right?

ELLIS: Twenty years.

CLIVEY: Twenty years.

[*MARY and CLIVEY look towards the baby. Pause.*]

Time flies.

[*Pause.*]

Well, I reckon we'd best be going, it's getting late, nearly time to get up I mean, and er... hey Mary would you hand me my crutch?

MARY: We can't just go!

CLIVEY: Why not?

MARY: This baby.

CLIVEY: It's not yours is it?

MARY: No but...

CLIVEY: Well then, you see I prefer to mind my own business.

MARY: Listen woman, this isn't a sack of potatoes, this is an infant you know. What are you going to do with it?

ELLIS: Don't start telling me. I'm a mother, I've been a mother longer than you've been able to walk.

MARY: You're sick, you ought to be in the hospital.

ELLIS: You ought to be back in prison.

MARY: That baby is very young. Give it to me. I can feed it.

ELLIS: No.

MARY: Can you feed it?

ELLIS: It's not hungry.

MARY: It's half dead.

ELLIS: It's having a rest. Don't please –

MARY: You don't know nothing.

ELLIS: Please I'll remember.

MARY: What have you got in your tits old woman? I've still got milk, you've got lager. Hand it over.

ELLIS: You haven't got milk.

MARY: They took my baby away because I bit the ear off a prison warder. I've been squirting it down the sink.

ELLIS: I don't want to lose my little boy again. I want to see if he recognizes me when he wakes up.

CLIVEY: You've probably changed a bit in the last twenty years, you might have to jog his memory.

ELLIS: He used to say mummummumum, mum.

CLIVEY: And what did you say?

ELLIS: I said, 'Where's your dad?'

CLIVEY: And what did he say?

ELLIS: In the pub. Dead at the bottom of the sea. Lying with his head in a dustbin somewhere, crushed, just like he crushed me.

CLIVEY: And then your baby just disappeared?

ELLIS: Someone walked off with him. She was probably not right in the head, the one that did it, but I forgive her. Or sane one minute and mad the next, that's probably what she was, the one that took him. She's probably sitting alone somewhere now behind a curtain with her tights hanging over the oven, wondering where her stolen baby boy has got to. She needn't worry.

MARY: Give him to me now.

ELLIS: I don't think he's warm enough. [*Hands him over.*]

MARY: He's cold...

ELLIS: You can't trust other people to look after your baby. And who ever helped anyone they didn't know to stay warm? Where's your baby?

MARY: In prison.

ELLIS: Yes, they lock them up young nowadays, stealing the milk probably, the little ones are devils for the milk. Are you going to give my son some of yours?

MARY: He won't wake up.

ELLIS: Yes, they're devils for the sleep as well. Shake him a little, gently. My mother used to shake me. And if we got wet she'd hang us over the oven to dry.

[*MARY starts crying silently.*]

Of course no amount of heat is going to keep a child happy. My mum was a bit over-anxious about the heat since it was never warm enough and we were always shivering. But she shouldn't have concentrated so much on it. I mean it's warm enough in here isn't it? It's summer. But that doesn't seem to keep him happy does it? He's cold anyway isn't he?

[*MARY sobs.*]

CLIVEY: What's going on?

MARY: It's dead.

CLIVEY: What?

MARY: The baby.

ELLIS: No amount of heat will keep him warm. He's stone cold isn't he?

MARY: Yes.

ELLIS: Whereas I think it's warm in here. Too warm. But he doesn't you see. People are different. [*Goes to the window.*] Why? What makes it so hot in here? It's like an oven. I'd rather be out there. [*Climbs to the window.*]

✱

[*A road, dark, orangey light, dark wind, cold ears, thin traffic PEDRO and MARTIN lumber along. PEDRO walking behind with stronger steps but his pace is hampered by a spasm which contorts his body. The essential of this spasm is a sweeping movement of the arm to the side and behind as if pushing something back that persistently approaches him from over his shoulder. 'Get back,' he mutters.*]

PEDRO: Wait. Do you know where we are?

[*MARTIN stops but keeps his head facing forwards. Pause. PEDRO's spasm.*]

Wait. [*Another spasm.*] Do you know where we are?
Eh? Martin, speak to me.

MARTIN: I had a bottle with shells in. He said it would
cure me.

PEDRO: Come on Martin please...Do you remember
what we're looking for? You don't know how a father
suffers. Just out having a good time while my wife
nurses our sick children, that's what you think. How
would you know? You've taken me on a wild fucking
goose chase.

MARTIN: The bottle broke on the beach. I looked for
my shells but there were too many.

PEDRO: I tell you, if we don't get the medicine soon
they'll die, how about that? Nothing impresses you
does it?

[*MARTIN gets out a small bottle of spirit and drinks.*]
Where did you get that? You didn't show me that?

MARTIN: Eh?

PEDRO: *Where did you get it?*

MARTIN: My sister. [*Hands it to PEDRO.*]

PEDRO: Eh? [*Laughs.*] Your what? [*Drinks.*]

[*MARTIN laughs in return.*]

You've got a sister?

[*MARTIN laughs some more enthusiastically.*]

Why didn't you tell me about that, eh?

[*MARTIN continues trying to laugh.*]

Stop bloody laughing!

MARTIN: I've got a sister. [*Tries to laugh.*]

PEDRO: All right. It's not funny any more. Where is she?

MARTIN: Here.

PEDRO: Where?

MARTIN: Here.

PEDRO: Keeps you happy does she?

MARTIN: Eh?

PEDRO: Your sister. Gives you booze, keeps you happy?

MARTIN: Yeah. [*Nods, smiles.*]

PEDRO: Why don't you take me to your sister? Why not eh? She on the bottle is she?

MARTIN: Yeah.

PEDRO: I bet she's a pretty sight.

MARTIN: Yeah.

PEDRO: Martin.

MARTIN: Mh?

PEDRO: Don't be stupid now, pay attention when I'm talking to you. [*Spasm.*] She make you like this?

MARTIN: No.

PEDRO: You are a weakling Martin. I won't let them touch you. Of course I might sell you. Wouldn't get much though because you couldn't do a good day's work could you? When did you last lift a finger to help yourself or anyone else? You have no sense of responsibility. You wander around like a ballerina. [*Spasm.*] Your life is a pirouette. [*Spasm.*] What have you done to me?

[*Utters three noises, hums, on the same note, a nervous sound, involuntary.*]

Voices.

[*Starts to cry for one second, stops.*]

Martin, I want to meet your sister.

I want to *meat* your sister, do you know what that means? I want to raise a finger to help her. [*Makes a gesture with his middle finger.*] I'm vulgar, I'm desperate. I'm the modern voice amongst the left-behinds. Listen, why don't you tell me about somewhere nice? There must be somewhere you'd like to be eh? There is isn't there?

[*MARTIN looks at PEDRO with a worried frown.*]

[*Puts his arm around MARTIN's shoulders.*] Come on Martin. I'm all right. I'm the nearest thing to a friend you'll ever get. I like secrets. I can keep them.

[*MARTIN offers PEDRO the bottle.*]

[*Takes bottle.*] This is the longest night of my life.

[*Hands it back.*] Your saliva is very sticky. I noticed it around the lip of the neck of the bottle you just gave me. And now I think about it you have little deposits of froth at the corners of your mouth. That's how we can all be sure you're not a baby, Martin. Babies don't drink or get dry. Do you know they take the brain cells from failed foetuses to heal the ailing skulls of the old? Watch out Martin. If you don't stop smiling like a foetus in a sink someone's going to make a long life out of you.

MARTIN: I stood on a piece of grass.

PEDRO: A piece of grass, by the kerbside was it?

MARTIN: ?

PEDRO: A piece of grass. Where the doggies go.

MARTIN: No.

PEDRO: Oh. Good. All right, come on.

MARTIN: A big road.

PEDRO: That's what I said.

MARTIN: Really big.

PEDRO: So you like motorways.

MARTIN: Yes.

PEDRO: Is there any more?

MARTIN: Mm?

PEDRO: Well what happened?

MARTIN: Nothing.

PEDRO: Nothing.

MARTIN: I like big roads, you can see the stars.

PEDRO: Oh yeah. [*Spasm. Notices a lump on the ground.*] What's that?

MARTIN: My sister.

PEDRO: I should have expected it. She's a mess Martin. Listen I didn't escape home and family for this...or did I? No, I didn't. My children lay dying. No, coughing, sweating, sneezing. They're probably delirious. And you just take me further away, further away. [*Looks at ELLIS.*] She's got an honest face. So have we all. All honest faces. Smile Martin. [*Spasm.*]

She's waiting for me now. Her face at the window. Counting the footfalls of all the ragged men going past our door stealing the milk. Maybe she'll throw herself out to them like a mad penguin into the icy sea. Or she might throw the babies out. So what's the matter with her [*ELLIS.*] then? Eh Martin?

MARTIN: She's resting.

PEDRO: And why is she resting?

MARTIN: Because her head is bleeding.

PEDRO: Is it? [*Looks.*] And why is her head bleeding?

MARTIN: Because she hit it on the ground.

PEDRO: Why did she hit it on the ground?

MARTIN: She was angry.

PEDRO: Really? No come on I bet she's not like that.

[*MARTIN gets out his binoculars.*]

I said I bet she's not like that! Martin.

[*MARTIN looks into the distance through binoculars.*]

You can't hide from it. Your sister lies bleeding at your feet. This isn't the first time. [*Spasm.*] And it isn't the last.

Where's the treasure eh?

[*MARTIN – binoculars.*]

Slumped sisters, blood on the paving stones. Binoculars. Where's the treasure chest?

MARTIN: There isn't any.

PEDRO: Can't you...[*Spasm.*] Can't you find it by the stars or something? [*Grabs him.*] Well go on, look! I didn't just come out here for a piss. For a walk in the warm wonderful air to shake my willy did I? [*Shouts.*] What have you got Martin!

[*MARTIN grasps his binoculars very tightly.*]

You're right. There's no reason to lose my temper. I want to get on with people, but I am trying to learn to insist on my own terms. I've had more fights in the past weeks...But otherwise I'd fade away. I want to look these people in the eye. Come on let's pick her up.

MARTIN: No.

PEDRO: Eh? You're right. Why pick her up? She's resting. People interfere because they want to take her soul home in their wallet.

Don't they? I'll keep them off. I'll hold them back...I'll lay down my body before the battering ram, and jam up the wheels, I'll do that for you Martin.

What's the matter Martin? You're crying. Real tears. Real tears. [*Dries them gently with his fingers.*] Martin, poor Martin. Look, I'll stroke her head. Like this.

MARTIN: She's cold.

[*PEDRO takes off his jacket and puts it over her. He strokes her hair softly. MARTIN sobbing violently. PEDRO goes to him.*]

PEDRO: Memories? Is it memories?

MARTIN: She fell off the oven. She tried to save me. Her feet got burnt. They smoked. Her blood was on the kitchen floor.

PEDRO: Your mother smoked you too much didn't she?

MARTIN: She tried to keep us warm.

PEDRO: She's still breathing anyway, she isn't dead.

[*MARTIN returns his binoculars to his eyes.*]

She isn't dead. That's something. [*Spasm.*] Isn't it Martin? Your sister is still alive and kicking.

We can stand on guard in case someone comes along and starts kicking her. They might try and sweep her up or something, eh? Put her in the trash can where she belongs, eh Martin? We'll put a stop to that. Life goes on. Doesn't it? We don't flinch.

[*Ambulance music, sirens, very loud engine noise, screeching of brakes, slamming of doors, croaking babble of radio. The ambulance has arrived. The ambulance crew come on. Played by the same actors as JOHNNY and LOUISE, in smart grey uniforms. PEDRO pushes MARTIN in front of ELLIS to hide her.*]

AMBULANCEMAN: Good evening sir.

PEDRO: Good evening.

AMBULANCEMAN: Everything all right is it?

PEDRO: Terrific.

AMBULANCEWOMAN: We've had reports of a body in the neighbourhood.

PEDRO: Ah.

AMBULANCEMAN: Yes. Have you seen one?

PEDRO: No, but I'll ask my friend if you like.

AMBULANCEWOMAN: We can do that thanks. [*Goes to MARTIN.*] Good evening sir.

[*No reply.*]

We've had reports of a person lying on the pavement. Have you seen anyone?

[*MARTIN puts his binoculars to his eyes.*]

It's all right, don't bother looking for it now. Did you see anyone before?

[*MARTIN points at PEDRO.*]

He was lying down was he?

[*MARTIN nods.*]

AMBULANCEMAN: Is that right sir? Were you lying down here?

PEDRO: Yes that's right.

AMBULANCEMAN: What for sir?

PEDRO: What for? Well you can't stay upright all the time, you'd end up falling over.

AMBULANCEWOMAN: I'm sorry, I didn't get that? [*Gets notebook out.*]

PEDRO: Listen, I don't want to keep you unnecessarily from your duties.

AMBULANCEMAN: You're not.

PEDRO: Oh.

AMBULANCEWOMAN: So what was it you said?

PEDRO: I said there's nothing to worry about, we're OK.

AMBULANCEWOMAN: Who is?

PEDRO: Me and Martin.

AMBULANCEMAN: Well we got called out to collect an unconscious body on the pavement. So we've got to get one, do you understand?

AMBULANCEWOMAN: We're not going back empty-handed.

AMBULANCEMAN: That's right. Now we're going to drive round a bit and see if we can spot anything.

AMBULANCEWOMAN: And if we don't spot anything we're coming straight back.

AMBULANCEMAN: All right?

AMBULANCEWOMAN: All right he said!

PEDRO: Yes that's fine.

AMBULANCEWOMAN: Listen we're not just out driving around for our own pleasure.

PEDRO: No.

AMBULANCEWOMAN: Denny, I don't like this geezer. He's sick.

AMBULANCEMAN: You've got to start getting used to them Lis. [*Lisa.*]

AMBULANCEWOMAN: He makes my fingers itch. He makes me want to get the stretcher out, know what I mean?

AMBULANCEMAN: I know exactly what you mean.

AMBULANCEWOMAN: I mean a transfusion or something.

AMBULANCEMAN: I know, I know, I was thinking exactly the same thing.

AMBULANCEWOMAN: I mean I want to start serving the public. Helping them. And this geezer, and this one, they need cleaning up. You know what I mean?

AMBULANCEMAN: All right Lis. We'll be back, all right?

[*AMBULANCEWOMAN pockets notebook. Points finger at PEDRO. They go. Ambulance noise and lights move away.*]

PEDRO: Well are we all still here? Look at her. [*Ellis.*] Does she look like someone you can save? Eh? [*Spasm.*]

[*MARY comes in carrying a large box carefully tied up with bits of string. CLIVEY follows on his crutches.*]

Ah it's you. I thought I heard giant's footsteps.

CLIVEY: I'm warning you!

[*MARTIN regards CLIVEY with his binoculars, CLIVEY stares back so MARTIN looks away.*]

PEDRO: Martin, look! There's the treasure we've been searching for all night. The chest. Just think, we can cart it round with us where ever we go. Hand it over.

MARY: You're mad, let go!

CLIVEY: Let go of that box you fucking nutter.

PEDRO: The Human Spider! You can't stand in the way of this. A box is a box. Martin and I are determined.

[*He pushes CLIVEY to the floor. CLIVEY lies on his back staring up at the sky, wordless.*]

MARY: No, you can't! There's a baby inside it!

PEDRO: A baby? Hear that Martin? What greater treasure could we have hoped to find? A human being with all its future ahead of it!

MARY: It's dead.

PEDRO: Dead? It will have to do. Hand it over.

MARY: [*Gives it to him.*] Take it then. I don't care. This woman had it. [*Indicates ELLIS.*]

PEDRO: Did she?

MARY: She must have dropped it or something.

PEDRO: Probably. These things happen. Did you make this box up?

MARY: Yes.

PEDRO: Why?

MARY: It had to be hidden somehow.

PEDRO: Don't worry.

MARY: I didn't kill it.

PEDRO: Good.

MARY: Nobody did. I've got a baby of my own.

I was in the middle of feeding it when they took it away from me. I'm going back to the prison now to look for it.

PEDRO: Prison. You won't find it there. They've given it to some Nice People by now. When you get there, look in the car park.

[*A blue light goes by silently. Everything freezes in the blue haze. MARY scurries away.*]

Look Martin, look what we've got here. [*Spasm.*] Do you think we'll get away with it? Look at these people! Between us all we've dropped this bouncing baby on the floor, we couldn't cope with it. We didn't have the equipment, not between us. And now it's dead.

[*MARTIN puts his binoculars to his eyes.*]

We'd better run. They'll get us. They're bound to get us for this. It's hopeless after all isn't it?

[*MARTIN just carries on looking through his binoculars. The music we've been hearing from a window up above gets louder and trafficky: out of the traffic sounds emerges the hooting and screeching of tyres and revving of engines, shouts of angry drivers. Enter JOHNNY and LOUISE escaping being run over.*]

JOHNNY: [*His arm around LOUISE's shoulder and guiding her to the kerb.*] Mind the cars, oops mind the cars mind the cars. Now, I quite agree with what you said just now: strength of mind is often in the legs.

LOUISE: Did I say that?

JOHNNY: The ability to walk, to go in the opposite direction. Now you've got strong white legs, if you could train them to take you in the other direction you'd be happy.

LOUISE: Are *you* happy?

JOHNNY: Am I happy?

LOUISE: Yes.

JOHNNY: Would you like to see my legs?

LOUISE: No I don't!

JOHNNY: No, come on I'll show them to you.

LOUISE: I want to sit down.

JOHNNY: Sit down? No! Keep moving! Now I'll be on the move until my washing is done then hopefully I will change into my dancing clothes and go on to a club somewhere. [*Shouts.*] Keep moving!

LOUISE: Clivey!

JOHNNY: No, keep –

LOUISE: There you are!

JOHNNY: My legs are white, like yours but thin. Bones. Like my eyes. Do you look in the mirror?

LOUISE: Where the fucking hell have you been?

JOHNNY: I'm sure you do. And what do you see there? All the way down and all the way up. That's not what I see. I see my bone eyes, my dreams. Can you smile? [*Pulls her round and makes her listen.*]

LOUISE: Course I fuckin' can!

JOHNNY: But in the mirror? Can you smile into the mirror at yourself, into your pavement eyes?

LOUISE: Leave off will ya – Clivey –

CLIVEY: You just left me on the floor, my legs got worse.

JOHNNY: Eyes of Scottish concrete.

LOUISE: But so have mine, I've started limping.

CLIVEY: Why's that then?

JOHNNY: They roll the roads at this time of night with little stones to make it easier for us all to tumble down to the bottom of the hills by daybreak.

LOUISE: My knees are like jelly.

JOHNNY: Daybreak is a happy time. [*Regards LOUISE.*] Lonely eyes but sociable fat legs, white and cold like dead chickens.

CLIVEY: Listen mate, shut up about her legs right! [*To LOUISE.*] You drink too much.

LOUISE: Where's your new girlfriend then?

CLIVEY: Leave it out Louise.

LOUISE: Did she get bored with you?

CLIVEY: Are you going to help me up? I'm in pain you know.

LOUISE: Yeah.

CLIVEY: Nobody thinks it's important because there's too much else going on. But what if it happened to you eh? You'd be like this lot – useless. You want to get yourself a pair of these. [*Crutches.*] At least I get about.

LOUISE: Yeah you get about all right.

CLIVEY: You think I look like a spider don't you, like this geezer does. You're afraid of me on these because I can move. You'd like me to sit on my arse like you. Like her! [*Points to ELLIS.*] Like all this lot, hopeless. Look at them all, just tilting towards that pavement. Eternal Sleep, that's what they want. Well not me. I like to be fast, I want a bit of pace. Do you get me

Louise, I can't hang around. I wouldn't like to see you in ten years' time. What a state! Can you pass me my crutch now please?

JOHNNY: You've broken the poor young lady's heart with your cruel words. Have you no mercy?

CLIVEY: Mercy? I can't even walk without sticks these days.

[*He goes out.*]

JOHNNY: Ah, foot strikes bleeding corpse. Who's this?

PEDRO: This is Martin's sister.

JOHNNY: Who's Martin?

PEDRO: This is Martin. He collects things in a jar, like Eeyore.

JOHNNY: [*Looking down at ELLIS.*] Has she jumped out of the window again? It must have got too hot for her. Come on, sit her up, get her legs moving.

[*PEDRO just stares at him with his head tilted back.*]

All right I'll do it myself.

[*JOHNNY pulls ELLIS up by her armpits to a sitting position and props her against a wall.*]

We'd better be careful though, those people who rode past just now nearly knocking me over, they're keeping watch for this sort of thing. We are not alone. No. They're going to roll our eyes into the gutter. And who's going to stop them eh? [*To PEDRO.*] I don't like your look. Do you want to come and try me eh?

PEDRO: [*Spasm, at which JOHNNY flinches.*] Weak arms. I've got weak arms. But I could always boot you in the balls. Couldn't I eh? [*Spasm.*] Martin. [*Limps over to MARTIN.*] Let me use those. [*Takes binoculars. Spasm.*

Looks up at the sky. To JOHNNY.] Forget about her.
Come and look at the Sun and the Stars. [*Pause.*]
Come on.

JOHNNY: All right, I will.

[*A blue light goes by silently. JOHNNY, forgetting the
question, starts looking about him, sees ELLIS and goes to
her again.*]

PEDRO: [*Trying to keep his attention.*] Look, look, Martin
and I were trying to find some er...treasure, we were
looking for treasure you know and em, we were
looking for a crate. Now It could have been up there,
up in the stars; listening? Or it could have been...well
under a pyramid. Or at the bottom of a wishing well.
Do you think we found any? Eh? Was that likely?
[*Shows him the box.*] Was it?

JOHNNY: I'm busy.

PEDRO: No, no, not busy. [*Spasm.*] Come on old cock,
spill the beans. What's the opinion? The answer isn't
in her fucking hair is it!

JOHNNY: I'm -

PEDRO: There's just blood in her hair, no answers up
there. Maybe you should look in her pants, or have
you already looked there?

JOHNNY: I'm a lonely man.

PEDRO: Don't start grovelling.

JOHNNY: Where did you get that?

PEDRO: It's something she dropped.

JOHNNY: It belongs to someone else I think. I think
Ellis found it didn't she, amongst some rubbish.

PEDRO: Who knows?

JOHNNY: It's just like her.

PEDRO: Is it?

JOHNNY: She might be in trouble I suppose.

PEDRO: Who isn't? [*Spasm.*]

[*JOHNNY goes to ELLIS and shakes her until she wakes up. A blue light goes past. We hear the ambulance motor idling as it crawls past.*]

JOHNNY: Ellis, wake up!

ELLIS: [*Exhausted.*] I can't move Johnny.

JOHNNY: Of course you can.

LOUISE: Come on love, lift up. [*Crouches down.*]

ELLIS: I can't, I can't I'm finished.

JOHNNY: Where've you been?

You look ill.

There's blood under your nose mixed with snot, it doesn't look very nice.

ELLIS: I'll wipe it.

JOHNNY: Your eyes have turned to water and your shirt's undone.

ELLIS: He returned from the sea, I thought he was buried in the depths. I wasn't ready. I was low, you know what I mean don't you Johnny?

JOHNNY: I don't know Ellis.

ELLIS: Then in a forgetful moment I told him I'd had a baby. 'Where is it?' he said. 'Where is it?' I said. 'Yes, where is it?' He was so angry. Isn't that peculiar? I promised I'd try to find it.

[*MARTIN turned the gaze of his binoculars upon her. She staggers up to him, and peeps underneath them until he lowers them.*]

Is that you?

PEDRO: Is that you Martin?

MARTIN: [*To PEDRO.*] Is that you?

PEDRO: This is your sister Martin.

ELLIS: Martin.

[*MARTIN smiles at her.*]

I saw you yesterday and I followed you. [*To the others.*] But he gave me the slip.

This is Turtle my brother. He goes on holiday to the seaside sometimes. Here it is, take it with you, I said, I can't bear it. Please Martin, little brother.

Of course I regretted it. I ran after him all the way down the dark paths, I couldn't find him...But I did, by the sound of the waves, I found him there bathing his feet in the foam in the dark with some box or other under his arm like treasure! 'Where's my baby?' I screamed. 'It's OK,' he said, poor Turtle, he'd left it someway up the beach safely with his own shoes, His Own Shoes!

PEDRO: [*Goes up to LOUISE.*] These are our last few moments together. Dance with me.

Tell me what you're doing here. Surely you could have waddled off after the Human Spider?

[*LOUISE shakes her head.*]

Then these are our last few moments together. Dance with me.

[*LOUISE shakes her head.*]

Come on, I'm longing for a little light relief. [*Tries to pick her up.*]

LOUISE: No, I can't.

PEDRO: Why not?

LOUISE: My legs.

[*PEDRO jerks her to her feet and hugs her to him, she hangs around him like a deadweight.*]

PEDRO: Right, this is it. Where's the music?

[*The ambulance arrives. A very loud engine noise and a siren, a blue light, slamming of doors, the ambulance crew come, played by the same actors as MARY and CLIVEY.*]

AMBULANCEMAN: Good evening, any trouble?

PEDRO: No.

AMBULANCEWOMAN: A caller said there were some people here unable to move.

PEDRO: Nonsense, we're all moving.

AMBULANCEWOMAN: What's the matter with her?

PEDRO: Who?

AMBULANCEWOMAN: The girl around your neck.

PEDRO: Oh her, she's very tired. [*Lets her drop to the ground.*] Look she's fallen asleep.

[*AMBULANCEMAN goes towards LOUISE, but PEDRO steps over her putting himself between LOUISE and the AMBULANCEMAN.*]

AMBULANCEMAN: Let's see.

PEDRO: She's doing fine. It's been a trying evening. You can examine me if you want. Here look into my eyes, my ears. Nothing but wax everywhere, I'm like a candle.

AMBULANCEMAN: Just calm down a minute. Let's have a look over here.

PEDRO: No, you can't, everyone's fine.

AMBULANCEWOMAN: Have I seen you before?

PEDRO: No. Listen tell me something, have you taken any children in tonight? They were very ill, they said the ceiling was purple, they said I was an evergreen...No?

[*AMBULANCEWOMAN shakes her head.*]

Maybe another ambulance?

AMBULANCEWOMAN: It's possible.

PEDRO: There seem to be a lot of them. [*Spasm.*]

AMBULANCEMAN: What?

PEDRO: Circling around.

AMBULANCEMAN: That's because we're looking for something.

PEDRO: What? [*Spasm.*]

AMBULANCEMAN: Show him the photograph.

AMBULANCEWOMAN: [*Shows him a photo.*] Seen it?

PEDRO: I...what is it?

AMBULANCEMAN: It's a box isn't it?

PEDRO: A box.

AMBULANCEWOMAN: Look there it is! [*Spies the box which PEDRO has put by ELLIS.*]

AMBULANCEMAN: Quick get it!

AMBULANCEWOMAN: Ha! This is it all right!

AMBULANCEMAN: Shake it and see.

AMBULANCEWOMAN: [*Shakes the box.*] Oh yes it couldn't be anything else.

AMBULANCEMAN: [*To PEDRO.*] Do you know what's in here?

PEDRO: Treasure. [*Spasm.*] Stolen I admit...But treasure all the same. What good is there in life if you can't strike it lucky every now and again eh?

AMBULANCEMAN: What if we ask these people over here?

PEDRO: Ask away.

[*PEDRO steps aside but then suddenly tries to strangle the AMBULANCEMAN who expertly elbows PEDRO's stomach and continues towards ELLIS, LOUISE and JOHNNY.*]

AMBULANCEMAN: [*To MARTIN.*] You've got a scar. It's a big'un. Who did that to you?

AMBULANCEWOMAN: His mother I bet.

AMBULANCEMAN: Your mother burn you up a bit did she?

AMBULANCEWOMAN: [*To JOHNNY.*] Can you help us do you think?

JOHNNY: Yes, I think so.

AMBULANCEWOMAN: [*Indicates ELLIS.*] Looks like this young lady here isn't capable of walking anymore.

JOHNNY: Yes, it looks that way certainly.

AMBULANCEWOMAN: [*Leaning to ELLIS.*] Hello love. All right are you?

[*ELLIS stares ahead of her.*]

She doesn't look well does she?

JOHNNY: No she doesn't.

AMBULANCEMAN: How about you, how are you feeling?

JOHNNY: I...I'm OK.

AMBULANCEWOMAN: How about if you come with her to keep her company?

AMBULANCEMAN: There that would be nice wouldn't it?

AMBULANCEWOMAN: You can hold the box.

AMBULANCEMAN: Know what's in it?

AMBULANCEWOMAN: You people don't know what you're doing do you?

AMBULANCEMAN: You're a bit of a plague. From the little one's point of view I mean.

AMBULANCEWOMAN: The children. Children aren't safe in your hands are they?

AMBULANCEMAN: It's a blooming crime what you've done between you.

AMBULANCEWOMAN: Look at the load of you.

AMBULANCEMAN: You're not really fit are you? Ask her, go on. Ya, you're not worth the trouble. Let's get the stretcher, take this lot away.

[*They go off to fetch stretchers. TINA comes on at the same time carrying JOHNNY's clothes to her chest.*]

TINA: [*Throwing the clothes to the ground.*] Here they are.

PEDRO: Martin, this is it, she's the treasure. Ask her her name.

MARTIN: [*To TINA.*] Look out!

PEDRO: My friend Martin here wants to go on a big
   road, where he can get a good look at the cosmos with
   his binoculars. [*Spasm.*] You look like a friendly
   harmless person. That's what he needs. Take him
   there go on.

   [*She walks away from him but he follows her grabbing her
   arm.*]

   [*Spasm.*] You're the caring type aren't you? You care.
   Don't you? Eh? [*Goes and drags MARTIN forward.*]

TINA: No.

PEDRO: There you are Martin, she doesn't care. But she
   will, work on her.

JOHNNY: You haven't washed these have you?

TINA: I'll do them I promise. Here give them. I forgot
   [*Takes them.*]

JOHNNY: It doesn't matter. Give them back.

TINA: [*Clutching them.*] No.

   [*TINA stumbles into ELLIS.*]

ELLIS: Was that your baby outside? I thought I
   recognized him.

TINA: Did you see him?

ELLIS: It's all right though. Help is on its way.

TINA: Is it?

ELLIS: They're bringing a stretcher.

TINA: Oh good.

ELLIS: They'll be here in a minute. I was a mother once.
   It isn't easy. When I dream about him we do this
   dance. He starts off really small like a little baby turtle

then he grows and gets as big as a dinosaur then he starts crawling across a map of the world until he ends bumping into these little planets with his little snout, out there in the cosmos.

PEDRO: Go on Martin take her hand!

JOHNNY: I'd give anything to be somewhere else. We haven't got long.

[*The AMBULANCE CREW returns carrying a stretcher.*]

PEDRO: Who's holding my hand? Here comes the battering ram.

✳

Downfall

CHARACTERS

HETTY

SECRETARY

WOMAN IN JAZZ PUB

RIGOLETTO

GERONIMO

WRITER

ROLO

POLICEMAN

VIOLENT MAN

MESSENGER

MADAME VANESSA, a fortune teller

MAN IN JAZZ PUB

MAN WITH GUN

CLANCY

CHARLIE

CARROL, a boy

ANITA

GIRLFRIEND

SPANISH LOVER

TOWER MAN, the man who climbed the Post Office Tower

Downfall was first performed at the Royal Court Theatre Upstairs, London on 6 July 1988. The cast was as follows:

HETTY SECRETARY WOMAN IN JAZZ PUB	Susan Brown
RIGOLETTO GERONIMO WRITER	Henry Goodman
ROLO POLICEMAN	Gerald Horan
VIOLENT MAN MESSENGER MADAME VANESSA (a fortune teller) MAN IN JAZZ PUB MAN WITH GUN	Des McAleer
CLANCY CHARLIE	Gary McDonald
CARROL (a boy)	Pearse Quigley
ANITA GIRLFRIEND SPANISH LOVER	Joy Richardson
TOWER MAN	Nabil Shaban

(the man who climbed the Post Office Tower)
MADAM VANESSA

DIRECTOR: Lindsay Posner
DECOR: Julian McGowan
LIGHTING DESIGN: Kevin Sleep
MUSIC: Stephen Warbeck

Part One

Part Two

Part Three

Part One

1. The Fortune Teller

[*CARROL and his GIRLFRIEND.*]

CARROL: I'm sorry.

GIRLFRIEND: Where have you been?

CARROL: I went to see a fortune teller.

GIRLFRIEND: What did he say?

CARROL: He didn't look at my hands at all. 'The whole world is in danger' he said. Then he walked off and left me standing in his tent. Am I late?

GIRLFRIEND: Late? Whatever for?

2. Corpse in the Garden

[*On the street, ROLO and HETTY. ROLO wears a smart velvety overcoat and a cheap open-necked shirt underneath. He has red-raw skin and an Irish face with blond hair and sideburns. He's been outside in the cold for years without ever once buttoning his coat, covering his neck or putting his hands in his pockets even though his wrists protrude enormously from his cuffs. His sideburns are golden and he carries a six pack.*]

[*Within hearing of a low-flying helicopter HETTY and ROLO are walking together. HETTY is hardly able to stand, her eyes are streaming. ROLO is supporting her as they progress slowly. They are talking, at first their words are inaudible.*]

HETTY: [*She tosses her head back and barks an ironic laugh at nothing in particular.*] Someone's trying to make a fool of me. The poison has gone out of everything, nothing tastes anymore.

ROLO: What do you think about that then?

HETTY: What?

ROLO: The man lying by his garden gate in a pool of blood.

HETTY: Eh?

ROLO: Let'g go back and take another look.

HETTY: Oh no, Rolo, I don't want to, I had such a hard time getting here in the first place. Take me home will you?

ROLO: You need a drink that's all.

HETTY: They hate me. Why do they hate me?

ROLO: Nobody hates you, no one even knows you exist.

[*A helicopter hovers a little way off.*]

3. Theatre, Manners and Money

[*'Casey Jones' burger bar, a railway station.*]

[*RIGOLETTO, an American training to be an Italian Director of Music, is on holiday in Britain.*]

[*CARROL sits opposite him.*]

RIGOLETTO: Listen, I used to write a fashion column for the *Chicago Tribune* you know but I stopped when they wanted me to write politics. Anyway, no one talks to anyone in Chicago anymore, they're too afraid of each other. It's terrible, but I was born there. So anyway I was telling you about my teacher right. Now he's training me but he's only doing it because

I'm so talented – does that sound conceited? I don't mean to be – And this man is *the* – well he is a great man. In fact he is the most famous musical star ever. But obviously he is also a great conductor otherwise he wouldn't be at the New York School of Music. I mean Britain has got the most marvellous schools, I've seen them, in fact before I conduct at Covent Garden I will do three years at the Guildhall School and they wrote me the most beautiful letter...anyway I have also this friend – I mean he's British – and, he was educated at Oxford University. In fact he is fiancéed to the daughter of the owner of *Time Magazine* and that's about as high as you can get, so he's beautifully connected and he's told me everything about the British educational system. So right now I know more about British culture than most of the people living there, I mean you know what I mean. So this friend of mine at Oxford has this other friend who owns a bank and is a great opera singer, who knows where the money is running in the world, not just in the States like Reagan does. So he really knows what's going to happen in Finance, Culture, Everything because it all starts from the top, that's where it's controlled from. He could tell you what the kids will be singing in fifteen years' time, those songs are already written...Listen the important thing to Americans is that Prince Charles's nails aren't properly manicured anymore; and the kids can see it in the photographs, and the unemployed can see that the people at the top are slothing off. In America we truly admire Britain and the British things you know. I've lived in Britain for five years, people need someone to look up to. We had John F Kennedy and everyone started looking clean and healthy, and then it started again with Carter, and now it's continuing with Reagan. Now Reagan you see was brought up in the whole theatrical thing, not legitimate theatre like *The Sound of Music* or Pirandello but at least where the value of good manners etc. were important, where you would find people like my friend the musical star...It's difficult to find these people, I mean the real theatrical people, even in Britain, but it's worth looking for them, they are still in control, they can help you if you want them to. They, really, are the future and not just in the theatre or even in the kind of music I want to conduct. You see none of the swing towards conservatism has surprised me because the people who are training me mind and body to become a conductor told me about it fifteen years ago because they know where the world's money is running, and that's where it's running at the moment because people really want change. In the USA everyone looks up to the theatre as something separate but as far as change is concerned that comes from...Direct from God, through the banks. [*Laughs.*] Drugs are out for example, you can't get drugs in New York anymore, they're right out, Reagan has stopped it, but it's been happening for years, they have abolished drugs in the United States. In Italy, you do drugs, you go to jail forever, in New York you're out in a day, but all that is being reversed. And the people are going to wake up and those at the top are going to have to take care of them because the old values of good manners and smart clothing will make it impossible for them not to do so. A friend of mine has a saying 'If you have no love you're on a bummer' and he had another one which they said about a Walt Disney film, *Fantasia* I think it was, that you can think you're right and if you have no love you'll be like a cymbal clashing and everyone will know you're wrong but if you keep right on at it you are going to be right in the end.

CARROL: Sounds like Bad news.

RIGOLETTO: No, it's good news.

4. Secrets

[*GERONIMO's office. GERONIMO, a member of the secret service, a chain smoking fanatic who works sixteen hours a day. His life is dominated by incurable stomach disease and chronic eye trouble, forcing him to change his spectacles every few minutes to no avail. A young black kid, CLANCY, sits opposite him.*]

GERONIMO: You won't find any friends here.

CLANCY: I'm sorry?

GERONIMO: You weren't trying to sell secrets?

CLANCY: I don't know any secrets.

GERONIMO: Everyone knows some kind of secret. In their hearts. Give me a cigarette.

[*Ring ring goes the phone.*]

Wait! What you have?

[*CLANCY empties his pockets then leaves.*]

5. Time, Space Odyssey, No Smoking

[*ANITA, a black girl, who has run away from home to King's Cross. She's overweight. She comes and sits at the table where RIGOLETTO and CARROL were sitting. But RIGOLETTO is no longer there.*]

CARROL: What did you make of that?

ANITA: [*No answer.*]

[*Long Pause.*]

Have you got a cigarette?

CARROL: [*Gives her one.*] Could you understand that?

[*She ignores the question.*]

[*Long pause.*]

I mean what...I didn't understand a word.

ANITA: He was right.

CARROL: What was he talking about?

ANITA: Time. Space Odyssey. That kind of think you know.

CARROL: Oh yeah. What do you reckon then?

ANITA: [*Ignores the question again.*]

CARROL: If you had a question of someone what would you ask them?

ANITA: I'd ask if they had a pound to lend me for a cheese burger.

[*Enter POLICEMAN.*]

POLICEMAN: Excuse me, there's no smoking in here.

CARROL: Sorry.

[*CARROL goes out after the POLICEMAN.*]

6. Wise Man in London

[*Outside the train station. A short speech to himself. Some way from the young POLICEMAN, who is standing, feet apart, surveying the noisy scene.*]

CARROL: [*To himself*] Excuse me officer, I hope you don't mind me asking but why –

Excuse me officer, but why –

[*Two NIGERIANS are standing talking by their suitcases.*]

CHARLIE: My uncle said to me – if you wish to become president of your country you have to leave the country and go and live in London. And then either come back as a very educated and wise man, or come back with arms. Either one you choose you can get it all organised in London.

7. Salt

[*Outside.*]

[*ANITA glides past.*]

CARROL: You'll get ill eventually if that's all you eat.

ANITA: I'm not fat.

CARROL: Chips don't make you fat, they –

ANITA: [*Interrupts*] Food isn't everything you know!

[*She goes.*]

8. Arms and Education

[*Outside the train station.*]

[*NIGERIANS, POLICEMAN, CARROL.*]

CHARLIE: He said the people here would be very willing to help with either arms or education. Of course they are normally polite but sometimes they don't quite realise the quantities of arms required by a developing nation. We need more than they do!

CARROL: [*To himself, rehearsing.*] Excuse me, constable, I don't want to upset you but would you mind telling me why?

[*The POLICEMAN walks off just as CARROL decides to approach him.*]

Surely I don't have to be a tourist to stand here?

[*RIGOLETTO appears at his side.*]

RIGOLETTO: 'Rigoletto' this isn't my real name you know, I got called this because of my hair. It used to be long and curly but when they asked me to write politics I cut it off. Of course it keeps growing. My friends say that I can't help being beautiful, however hard I try. I notice you're not wearing a coat. You should be wearing a long overcoat, and you should go to a hairdresser's. In Chicago it used to mean you were a bohemian. People looked up to you.

CARROL: It wouldn't mean that here.

RIGOLETTO: Listen, in a few years all those words like Hippie, Yuppie, Death Squad will all be gone and then you'll be respected for the true artist you really are.

CARROL: Thank you.

9. The Spanish Lover, Love Cannot Blossom

[*The SPANISH LOVER, a black girl, is dressed in filthy rags and erotic clothes. She is tied to a chair.*]

[*CARROL strolls into view in front of her and smiles at her.*]

SPANISH LOVER: You're really very charming you know, so disingenuous, so enigmatic. You're all I've ever wanted.

CARROL: Thank you. I fancied you as soon as I saw you.

SPANISH LOVER: You like this kind of thing? You know you can't touch me don't you?

CARROL: Yes, I know.

SPANISH LOVER: You would like to wouldn't you?

CARROL: Yes, of course.

SPANISH LOVER: It's so difficult to tell these days.

CARROL: Love cannot blossom.

SPANISH LOVER: No kisses.

CARROL: I could kiss your ankles.

SPANISH LOVER: No, I have an open sore. These shoes.

CARROL: Better not then.

SPANISH LOVER: Your sweet words instead then.

CARROL: My sweet words. [*Embarrassed.*] You know, it isn't love.

SPANISH LOVER: You don't have to explain if you don't want to.

CARROL: I don't mind. Look when all this is over...

SPANISH LOVER: I'll always be your Spanish Lover anyway.

CARROL: I mean it though, I'll come back and we'll –

SPANISH LOVER: We'll touch.

CARROL: You look so beautiful –

SPANISH LOVER: Goodbye.

CARROL: When all this is over...

[*The SPANISH LOVER disappears.*]

❖

Part Two

10. A visit from Madame Vanessa

[*CARROL has gone to see MADAME VANESSA, a fortune teller* (who is the TOWER MAN in disguise). *Behind MADAME VANESSA sits a person whose face is hidden by a newspaper.*]

MADAME VANESSA: Have you paid?

CARROL: Yes.

MADAME VANESSA: Alright then.

CARROL: The poster said you can give predictions.

MADAME VANESSA: [*Looks at CARROL long and hard.*] Wait there, I have to make a phone call.

[*Goes out.*]

[*Pause. CARROL waits.*]

[*The person lowers her newspaper. It is ANITA.*]

11. Amphetamines

[*The VIOLENT MAN is standing upright and very still. He is old looking with an emaciated face and body. He has a walking stick for an injury and holds a bottle of cider loosely by his side. He is staring with a mild stare at the kerb of the pavement opposite. He speaks softly. CARROL is walking along.*]

VIOLENT MAN: Excuse me could you help me by telling me where I can find Wilberforce Road?

CARROL: I think it's up there.

VIOLENT MAN: Do you want a drop of this?

CARROL: No, I feel bad enough as it is.

VIOLENT MAN: I see my doctor there.

CARROL: Is it for your leg?

VIOLENT MAN: No, it isn't for my leg. That happened yesterday when I was thrown under a car on the Camden Road.

CARROL: Oh.

VIOLENT MAN: He gives me the pills I need you see, the amphetamine pills you know otherwise I wouldn't be very well at all without them. [*He smiles.*]

[*CARROL nods.*]

He gives me now, it is em...well fifteen pills he gives me every day.

CARROL: No wonder you look ill.

VIOLENT MAN: Em...yes I suppose you might have a point there. But look at my face, look into my eyes. Don't I look like a psychopath?

CARROL: A bit.

VIOLENT MAN: There you see. I'm a very violent man. Don't tell anyone about this doctor now.

CARROL: No, I won't.

VIOLENT MAN: Are you alright for a bit of money?

CARROL: What?

VIOLENT MAN: Do you need any cash, I can give it to you.

CARROL: No thanks, I'm alright.

12. The Post Office Tower, 32 f.p.s.

[*A street.*]

[*TOWER MAN, the man who climbed the Post Office Tower,
HETTY and ROLO.*]

TOWER MAN: Stop moaning and bloody crying!

HETTY: Shut up!

TOWER MAN: [*He declaims.*] Silence please. I would like
to start by saying that I'm freezing cold. But!

[*A helicopter far off.*]

...they say it is a lot colder at the top of the post office
tower. Give me a drink will you. Who wants a cigarette?

HETTY: Stop bloody shouting! Who are you shouting at?

TOWER MAN: Pardon?

ROLO: We're right here in front of you.

TOWER MAN: Oh yes, but other people want to hear as
well, do you mind?

[*Clears throat.*]

I was tumbling past the 32nd floor when I heard the
telephone ringing. And I said as I hit the deck: 'I'm not
the last person on earth, because I heard the telephone
ring as I flew past the offices on the 32nd floor'.

'But it might have been an alarm call', said the
ambulance man as he picked me up off the pavement.

'What? At this time of the day?' I said. 'Don't be such
a bloody fool!'

HETTY: Make him shut up Rolo. I've got a headache.

13. Which side are you on?

[*GERONIMO's office.*]

[*CLANCY is sitting.*]

GERONIMO: If you are not for me you are against me!

This isn't a matter for public discussion!

How do you expect me to do my job. If you think this is sinister you should see what the other side get up to! We've been doing this since Anglo-Saxon times and we're not going to stop now!

Don't look around for help. You're alone in this room. Anyone in a room with me is alone.

Look into my eyes. I've never done any more wrong than you have.

Now. Which side are you on?

14. The only cure for Loneliness, from Arsenal to Guatemala

[*A street.*]

HETTY: How dare you!

TOWER MAN: What a haughty woman!

[*To HETTY.*] You act as if you are drunk.

HETTY: [*Threatening a can.*] Do you want this in the side of your skull?

TOWER MAN: I warn you I'm fearless. I've been hit more times than you could possibly imagine. I live here, I live just around the corner. The shops and the buildings are small and sweet just as they were when I first arrived as a seventeen-year-old girl from across the sea. Yes I live in Arsenal where there is a well-known cult of being English, one day I shall burn it down. [*To ROLO.*] Where do you live?

ROLO: Here and there.

TOWER MAN: Really?

ROLO: Aye.

TOWER MAN: Aye. Three times divorced?

ROLO: Never married.

TOWER MAN: Never?

ROLO: Well. Once.

TOWER MAN: Once. Once is enough, if you're the bachelor kind. Is this woman your ex-wife?

ROLO: No, she's not.

HETTY: [*With a toss of her head.*] Oh God!

TOWER MAN: What did she say? What a bitter remark. And that Galway toss of tne head we all know so well. What sorrowful years we have all lived together! And could live again still if we only wanted. In a great big family. After all it's the only defence against loneliness.

[*To HETTY.*] Don't think I don't appreciate a good woman when I see one. No, no I can see by your teeth and your fine legs that you were once a great beauty on a small scale. Do you think I have no experience with dancing and kissing and that kind of thing?

HETTY: I don't care if you do or you don't.

TOWER MAN: Come on.

HETTY: Don't please touch me!

TOWER MAN: I was out walking with my true love. A small Irish man like yourself, in a dark blue suit and a red face, walking home said 'hello' to us without looking for a reply. Our voices, too, greeted him and the sound rang out into the cold night air and everything was sweet. – But! Moments later I was struck down in a fight over God knows what. Someone had their feet struck out across the way, I stumbled etc., then he said the woman I was with had coughed all over him, well, I couldn't stand for that.

ROLO: What did you do?

TOWER MAN: I allowed him to beat me. But, offended by my boldness, he tried to rob me as well. I think he was a member of the secret services. He had a little phial in his breast pocket which he took out and then poured the contents all over my hands. 'This will teach you. It's called the Kiss of Death; You are the Nigger of the World.' I expect to die a long and painful death one day. And she, I believe, is working for the other side these days. Things change so quickly, that side will soon be this side and they'll welcome me home even though I won't have been anywhere.

ROLO: Isn't that the same as us! We never go anywhere.

TOWER MAN: Here take this.

ROLO: What is it?

TOWER MAN: A photograph of Guatemala. I bet they don't know which side they're on either.

[*The TOWER MAN takes up a copy of the National Geographic and rips out the pages one by one dropping them to the floor.*]

15. The Writer's Prophecy

[*A street.*]

[*A WRITER accompanied by a smart woman, his SECRETARY, bumps into CLANCY.*]

CLANCY: Go ahead, rob me man, I haven't got anything.

WRITER: I'm not going to rob you.

CLANCY: Oh yeah, we'll see.

WRITER: No, no, you misunderstand me. I'm a writer. Look here's my portable typewriter, and this is my amanuensis.

CLANCY: Oh yeah.

[*The SECRETARY listens, rapt.*]

WRITER: Governments are unfit to govern. The world is hurtling towards 100 disasters and they are always the last to take it into consideration. The day will come when I, too, will become a leader of men – on that day I hope you'll stop listening to what I'll be saying, I'll have marks on my shoulders and on the backs of my hands.

[*To CLANCY.*] Do you want to hear about the time I went to Southend?

CLANCY: No.

WRITER: I went to Southend and ate in a café on the front. The meat was off but I only realised by the last bite. So I crossed the road and stood with my bare feet in the ice-cold foam and vomited it back into the sea with all the other sewage. That's what you have to do with life. Move on from the old to the new. There's nothing to be sentimental about. People's lives are eaten up with anguish they don't dare utter, even to themselves. What's holding us back? Mainly just elaborate dreams of committing some small crime; as if that would make everything better.

CLANCY: [*Who has had his fingers down his throat.*] Listen, I've been robbed more times than you could possibly imagine.

WRITER: I expect you have.

CLANCY: I've been mugged you know.

WRITER: Mm.

[*The SECRETARY stares at the WRITER admiringly.*]

CLANCY: One time I was in a bank and these geezers came running in with hoods over their heads and guns and took all my money.

WRITER: That was bad luck. Do you know where we are?

CLANCY: Sure. We're standing right in the middle of the road.

WRITER: That's right. And if we didn't make a conscious decision we'd stay here. Until eventually we got run over by someone in a fast car who didn't feel like stopping.

[*The SECRETARY is impressed. She glows. He glows.*]

CLANCY: I've never met anyone with hair like yours. How do you get it to stay like that?

WRITER: What, you mean curly like this?

CLANCY: Yeah, it must be a wig right?

WRITER: No, it isn't.

CLANCY: Tell me then.

WRITER: I soak it.

CLANCY: What in?

WRITER: I couldn't tell you that.

CLANCY: Why not?

WRITER: No.

16. Notes for a Novel

[*GERONIMO's office. The WRITER's SECRETARY.*]

GERONIMO: And what else did he make you do?

SECRETARY: My job was to read all the newspapers and to scour them for labels to hang around people's necks.

GERONIMO: And why did you have to do that?

SECRETARY: It was for his book.

GERONIMO: What was it?

SECRETARY: A novel. A sort of social criticism called 'When Walls Collide'.

GERONIMO: Did you read it?

SECRETARY: Yes, while I typed it out.

GERONIMO: What was your opinion of the book?

SECRETARY: Do you mind if I take my coat off?

17. Some Introductions are made

[*A street. ROLO. HETTY is lying in the gutter.*]

[*ROLO picks up HETTY from the ground, gives her a can of beer and stands beside her. He offers CARROL a can.*]

CARROL: No thanks I feel bad enough already.

ROLO: Hetty needs a drink. Christ she's an important woman.

HETTY: Let go of me!

ROLO: Jesus, you know she's so important she can't stand up.

HETTY: Let go of me now!

ROLO: Do you know she once had a full set of teeth? She had them all pulled out at the age of thirty-two because she thought they weren't straight. And her legs are ruined because she had the varicose veins stripped right out of them, all just for the sake of vanity.

HETTY: Will you shut up and help me to fucking stand properly.

ROLO: She thinks I have another woman.

HETTY: [*In tears of frustration.*] Of course he has, look at him; he looks twenty even though he's thirty-eight and I look like an old woman and I'm only forty-two!

ROLO: That's the luck of the draw, what do I care? But try explaining that to her. Anyway she can't do it anymore. Did you ever try talking to a woman about true love?

CARROL: No.

ROLO: They have a more mechanical view of things. Now if Hetty only knew how I like the look of her. We boys are the romantics.

HETTY: [*To CARROL, stroking his face.*] Don't worry if you've got nothing to say to us. We understand.

18. Down a Dark Alley

[*GERONIMO and CLANCY down a dark alley. CLANCY is wearing a blond wig.*]

GERONIMO: I think you've missed the point.

CLANCY: I'm just trying to get home.

GERONIMO: Come and sit down here, I want to explain something.

[*CLANCY doesn't move.*]

GERONIMO: You see I have a deep longing to solve problems. I want to be useful to the world. I get the feeling you don't particularly care.

CLANCY: [*Silence.*]

GERONIMO: And I feel angry, that's another thing. Senseless, violent behaviour for example, makes me...well I can't understand it. It gives me a strange feeling inside. If things could be organised with the necessary minimum of control there wouldn't be any opportunity. I'd like to help towards that end, that's all. Man has a dark heart, you can see it in me, I can see it in you. But I am channelling my energies into crushing that darkness. What do I see when I look at you? I just see potential for disruption, for upsetting. If you could you'd destroy me wouldn't you? And I wouldn't look to your kind for any mercy either...Whereas I can tolerate you so long as I can be sure you'll behave. So. What is it to be? Do you understand me?

CLANCY: No, I don't understand you and I want to go.

GERONIMO: You won't even listen even though I've taken the trouble to explain it all reasonably.

CLANCY: I want to get out of here!

GERONIMO: What's the wig for?

CLANCY: It's to protect me from being robbed.

GERONIMO: It's not going to protect you. How are your legs? Do they walk OK?

CLANCY: Yes, they walk fine.

GERONIMO: You'd do less harm if you had a kind of limp.

CLANCY: Do you think so?

GERONIMO: I think so.

19. The Querrent receives a City Saver

[*CARROL is at the fortune teller's. ANITA is no longer there. The VIOLENT MAN is dressed as MADAME VANESSA and has taken her place. He hands something to him.*]

CARROL: What's that?

MADAME VANESSA: A City Saver.

CARROL: Thanks.

MADAME VANESSA: Travel is so expensive these days.

20. The Train Departs Tomorrow

[*CARROL is sitting in a train station near a platform. ANITA comes along. She has several coats and jumpers wrapped round her shoulders. But only one pair of tights covering her legs and ankles. She has a deep cough, she's been cold for a long while. She goes past.*]

CARROL: I'm waiting for a train.

[*ANITA turns and looks at him. Then walks on coughing.*]

CARROL: [*After her.*] I've just seen that policeman. I think he's following me.

ANITA: This is his beat.

CARROL: You don't like me do you?

ANITA: How could I, I don't even know you.

CARROL: I bought you a fucking cheese burger.

ANITA: Thanks.

CARROL: I don't want gratitude.

My train departs tomorrow.

[*ANITA nods vaguely.*]

CARROL: What's it like being cold?

ANITA: It's alright.

CARROL: Yes, it leaves tomorrow morning. I'll stay here until then.

ANITA: Why don't you go home and wait for it.

CARROL: I don't like small rooms with low ceilings. I lose all sense of proportion so a person could seem to be only an inch high, do you know what I mean?

ANITA: Yeah.

CARROL: You have to stick your head out of the window and try to focus on something across the road.

ANITA: Yeah, I know.

CARROL: And then everything is returned to normal size.

ANITA: Yeah.

CARROL: Really?

ANITA: Mmm.

CARROL: Yeah. It's like falling isn't it?

21. On the Run

[*A helicopter swoops in upon its prey. A searchlight illuminates the VIOLENT MAN as he struggles along. He stops, freezes, slowly raises his eyes to look above him.*]

22. Ħetty walks but meets an Immovable Object

[*HETTY tries to walk. Sound of a helicopter nearby.*]

[*She veers incredibly.*]

[*Veers more. Reaches an immovable object.*]

[*She's stuck.*]

HETTY: Help me.

[*Falls down.*]

HETTY: Oooo!

[*Lies in silence.*]

[*Sounds of a helicopter coming nearer.*]

HETTY: Help me.

23. Tomorrow is 2½ hours

[*The SPANISH LOVER. The VIOLENT MAN comes before her.*]

VIOLENT MAN: I suppose you don't recognise me.

SPANISH LOVER: No, I don't.

VIOLENT MAN: The years have played tricks on my body and my face. I'm not myself any more. I've sold parts of my body, I can unscrew my teeth.

SPANISH LOVER: Your skin looks like a shroud, whoever you are.

VIOLENT MAN: I managed to keep only the part of me you hated. That wouldn't be given away.

SPANISH LOVER: Are you young?

VIOLENT MAN: Thirty-seven.

SPANISH LOVER: You look sixty.

VIOLENT MAN: Do I?

SPANISH LOVER: Disease has got a hold over me as well.

VIOLENT MAN: I've travelled many miles to be with you tonight.

SPANISH LOVER: Why tonight?

VIOLENT MAN: I couldn't get any medicine.

SPANISH LOVER: I can't help you.

VIOLENT MAN: I wasn't expecting –

SPANISH LOVER: Are you ill?

VIOLENT MAN: I don't, I don't...people's faces, I can never predict what's going to happen.

SPANISH LOVER: What did happen?

VIOLENT MAN: Tonight? I came here.

SPANISH LOVER: Do you have anything to drink?

VIOLENT MAN: Do you – ?

SPANISH LOVER: I look different as well don't I?

VIOLENT MAN: Yes.

SPANISH LOVER: The world isn't going to help us get together again.

VIOLENT MAN: No...

SPANISH LOVER: Do you think we got off lightly?

VIOLENT MAN: I don't know.

SPANISH LOVER: Come and see me again.

[*The VIOLENT MAN walks to the window and looks out into the night.*]

VIOLENT MAN: How many hours is it until tomorrow?

SPANISH LOVER: 2½.

VIOLENT MAN: That should be alright.

Part Three

24. Ᵽiding

[*The deafening sound of a helicopter flying low, hovering overhead. A searchlight discovers the VIOLENT MAN. He falls to the ground to hide himself.*]

[*The helicopter continues to hover.*]

25. The Tables Turning

[*An office.*]

[*The WRITER's SECRETARY and GERONIMO, in shorts. He sits. She stands behind his chair.*]

GERONIMO: I've pushed fear to the limit. I've made the whole world chomp on the bit.

SECRETARY: What do you expect, gratitude?

GERONIMO: Respect, sympathy. Love for an old man at the end of his career. I do a job just like everyone else...I laid my heart to waste in the service of society – somebody has stolen my uniform. I have to wear these stupid fucking shorts. Was it you?

[*Pause.*]

Is this it? Am I under arrest?

SECRETARY: Not yet. You're not a creative man, understand! We've got you for that murder by the way.

GERONIMO: What murder?

SECRETARY: Cold blooded. You killed a pillar of society.

GERONIMO: I didn't.

SECRETARY: Remember a little room in North London, a doctor's surgery.

GERONIMO: No.

SECRETARY: The one who wrote false prescriptions. Then you let another man take the blame for what you did.

GERONIMO: When was this?

SECRETARY: [*Looks at her watch.*] About five minutes ago.

GERONIMO: That's impossible!

SECRETARY: Who cares. You have no alibi.

GERONIMO: I was here with you, planning to fly to Miami.

SECRETARY: Forget it. How many murders have you committed? Countless. We've made it just right for you, tailor made. You wouldn't want a sex offence?

26. The Train Platform

[*Train platform. The VIOLENT MAN is nervous. His body is jerking around, his legs are weak at the knees.*]

VIOLENT MAN: [*He lets out some grunts, in rapid succession, tapping his foot very quickly, slapping his sides with his arm.*] Huh, huh, huh, huh, huh, huh, huh, huh, huh, aaah!

CARROL: [*He's just got off the train, he holds his railway ticket in his hand.*] What's going on?

[*VIOLENT MAN turns his head, looks at him.*]

[*CARROL starts a question he daren't ask.*]

[*VIOLENT MAN runs at CARROL his limbs all out of

control. He grabs him as if he's throwing his whole body at him, his head nodding and his leg stamping.]

[*CARROL taken aback.*]

VIOLENT MAN: [*Stepping a half step back, breathing hard.*] Do I recognise you?

CARROL: [*Searching for something to say.*] You gave me some money —

VIOLENT MAN: Did I? Did I? [*He puts his head down in his sleeve.*]

CARROL: You offered me —

VIOLENT MAN: What, what!

CARROL: Money!

VIOLENT MAN: Did I?

CARROL: Yes! You gave me money...for this ticket...Look! [*Shows him his red railway ticket.*]

VIOLENT MAN: For this?

CARROL: Yes. [*Breathless.*] We met...I don't know how. I was on my way to the station, you just gave it to me.

VIOLENT MAN: Why did I do that?

CARROL: I can't...explain, I don't know.

VIOLENT MAN: Who are you?

CARROL: No one.

VIOLENT MAN: Do you know me?

CARROL: No...yes.

VIOLENT MAN: Can you remember me?

CARROL: Yes.

VIOLENT MAN: What was I like?

CARROL: What were you like...you were...

VIOLENT MAN: [*Desperate.*] Tell me quickly!

CARROL: You were alright! You were! You were alright!

VIOLENT MAN: Wh...Wh... [*Unable to ask. Jerkily shaking his head in a kind of disbelief.*]

27. A Train Got Lost

[*CARROL's GIRLFRIEND standing alone. Waiting. Playing with her fingers anxiously.*]

[*CLANCY comes along. He still has a blond curly wig.*]

CLANCY: Something's gone wrong.

[*He staggers carefully towards her.*]

A train has got lost in a tunnel somewhere. It went into the tunnel, got smaller and smaller...and then...

GIRLFRIEND: What train?

CLANCY: A train. You know, from a station.

Look, I'm wearing a wig, can you tell?

[*Turns out his pockets.*] I haven't got any money. I've got this instead. If someone decides to rob me they can take my hair.

Do you want to know how I get it to stay like this? I soak it. It helps too because I'm on the run from the police. They want me for a Building Society job, they say they've got me on video. I keep telling them it was *my* money the people took but they don't believe me. Do you believe me? You should do girl. Who was it took everything? Was it me; or was it someone else? I'm getting thinner and thinner. I go on trips to the seaside. What are you waiting for?

GIRLFRIEND: My boyfriend.

CLANCY: Your boyfriend. Well I can take his place. What's he like?

GIRLFRIEND: [*Thinks about him.*] He's lost.

CLANCY: Well then, so am I. And what's more someone pushed me under a car. My legs. Well. My legs. It doesn't hurt you know but I can't corner very quickly. I'm no good at chasing.

GIRLFRIEND: Leave me alone now, boy, I want to think.

CLANCY: Maybe he's tired of you. Come on. I'll let you run your fingers through my hair if you promise not to steal it. There are so many people in the world. If you can't help one you might as well help another. It can hardly matter which of them can it? Your boyfriend isn't here. I am. I have pain. [*He demonstrates a short groan.*] Look. [*A longer groan.*]

Quick, quick, quick, quick, quick, quick, quick, quick.

[*He launches into a cacophony of groaning which develops into shrieking.*]

28. Trying to Run

[*The helicopter seems to swoop down. The VIOLENT MAN despite being disabled by his leg is trying to run away, but the surging of the craft above forces him to dodge and swerve and to be doubled up.*]

29. In the Garden of Skullduggery

[*The man who climbed the Post Office Tower is imitating himself climbing on a rooftop. He holds a speech.*]

[*ROLO stands below. HETTY lies supine.*]

TOWER MAN: The wind came and brought us blizzards of snow. Which stayed a while, froze us, brought us to our knees.

Then came the fiercest of the fierce winds that blows us back along the streets and freezes the very blood in our sores.

But for all its knocking and roaring it has blown the snow away off the roofs again and off the gutter's kerbside edge...away down the drain.

Thanks be to God.

ROLO: Come down from there.

TOWER MAN: Someone said they thought they saw me climbing on the roof of a school. I don't deny it...I went there to watch the children play. But the dinner ladies had lined them all up against the wall in silence.

What does it all mean? That's what they all asked as I returned to ground level.

[*He climbs down to ROLO.*]

What does it all mean? [*He weeps.*]

ROLO: I don't know.

TOWER MAN: We are three adventurers searching for occupation. Keep that end in sight. The horse beneath the sea, the ship upon the mountain.

ROLO: We're three alcoholics.

TOWER MAN: I'm not feeling well. Perhaps death is near, perhaps I only have the simple flu. But it's a bad one. [*Sits by HETTY's head.*]

[*ROLO continues to stand. His red-raw wrists showing from his sleeves. He smokes a cigarette.*]

TOWER MAN: Why is this woman so fast asleep?

ROLO: She isn't. She's listening, planning her next move, she's awaiting arrest.

TOWER MAN: Maybe we should kneel and pray. If this is her garden of skullduggery. Shall we carry her off away from here? Does she want the cup to pass from her lips?

ROLO: I think the cup has finally passed her lips once too often.

TOWER MAN: They normally come in the early morning. She doesn't look as if she'll be too fresh. They may be armed. They may try to shoot her legs off if they're feeling nervous. Best try to wake her up.

[*ROLO just stares down at her.*]

[*The TOWER MAN makes no move towards her. Pause. He moves to go.*]

TOWER MAN: The gates are closing, the boats are pulling away from the harbour.

[*Pause.*]

Will you still be standing here when I get back?

ROLO: [*No cigarettes left in his box.*] Have you got a spare cigarette?

TOWER MAN: Yes. [*Searches an empty packet.*] Look, someone smoked them all.

[*ROLO turns round and picks up an old one.*]

TOWER MAN: Right then.

[*TOWER MAN leaves. ROLO stands boldly over the sleeping HETTY. His red-raw wrists showing in the cold air.*]

30. Ĥope for the Future. Very Exciting

[*WRITER and SECRETARY.*]

WRITER: This is very exciting. I feel as if something is going to change. How long have people been pushing the stone to the top of the hill, how many rebels have there been, how many have died in front of the wall?

[*Pause.*]

What happens to me is immaterial. In another couple of years, I might not even still be writing. I might give it up, or find something else to do. I'm not pretending to anyone that I was born to do this.

SECRETARY: Is that it for today?

WRITER: Yes. Do you want to stay tonight?

SECRETARY: [*Looks at her watch, considers.*] Em......

31. The Ledge

[*The TOWER MAN alone.*]

TOWER MAN: A ledge or a lump on the wall?

We wouldn't normally call a tiny piece of plaster sticking to one of the tiles in the bathroom a ledge, but rather a lump.

A ledge would normally be something a human being could stand on to save him falling down a cliff face.

32. The Messenger Arrives

[*ROLO, HETTY and the TOWER MAN standing in a street.*]

[*A MAN rushes in gasping for breath. He stands panting at least twenty times while the others are waiting.*]

ROLO: What is it?

MAN: I... [*Pant etc.*] I...I...

ROLO: Spit it out.

MAN: I just ran down...down the...Euston Road...[*Coughs, nearly chokes.*]...I had to...I had to...[*Collapses, lies on the ground, they loosen his collar.*]...a message...

ROLO: Who was the message from?

MAN: ...a message...

ROLO: What was it?

[*ROLO lights a cigarette.*]

[*MAN stops panting, goes silent.*]

HETTY: Is he dead?

ROLO: I don't know.

HETTY: Sure to God I wish *I* was dead!

ROLO: Look, he's moving!

[*Helps him up.*] There you go. Stand there. Take it easy now.

MAN: I ran all the way down Euston Road. I had to find you I had to tell you what the message was.

TOWER MAN: Well, what was it?

[*The MAN just stands shaking his head slowly and regretfully.*]

[*End of the first half.*]

❖

Part Four

33. Something is Amiss

[*The TOWER MAN alone.*]

TOWER MAN: The vulture has landed – something is amiss. I went home to find the shops all closed and the doors of the empty churches wide open! People were running about screaming – 'It's Sunday. It's Sunday!'

'Is God going to help us?' I asked them. No one knew what I was talking about.

The world could be a far better place.

34. The Bleeding Policeman

[*The VIOLENT MAN is lying on the floor, after a long chase with the helicopter. HETTY is standing by him. She is sober.*]

[*The VIOLENT MAN is breathing very hard. He stops panting, lifts his head and looks. He tries to talk but only a tense groan comes out which he is dissatisfied with and turns into a shout from the stomach and throat.*]

HETTY: Looks like they caught you. You're like a dog now.

VIOLENT MAN: What are you doing?

HETTY: I am enjoying a rare moment of soberness. I'm watching the lorries' lights go by at eye level.

VIOLENT MAN: Can you help me?

HETTY: No.

[*Sighs.*]

No this isn't a moment of clarity, this is the opposite.

[*Watches some lights go by.*]

Brmm, brmm.

VIOLENT MAN: Why don't they come the bastards.
They want to watch me sweat.

[*He shouts in pain.*]

HETTY: 'Are you hurt?'

VIOLENT MAN: Give me something to drink.

HETTY: 'Where are your persecutors?'

[*VIOLENT MAN gurgles in pain.*]

HETTY: 'Your whole body seems to be giving you
trouble.' You need a bloody drink.

VIOLENT MAN: Have you got one?

HETTY: I haven't got one. Where are they then? If you
try to get away they'll come alright. Have you been
waiting long for this? I have. It's me next.

[*The VIOLENT MAN jerks himself up to a sitting position.
His face is ashen and his breathing is heavy.*]

HETTY: I heard them chasing you. Were you doing a lot
of shouting? No? Someone was. I heard shouting the
whole time. Lots of people it must have been, all
together. It sounded like a football match. Great roars
of anger. The police don't roar with anger do they? It
wasn't you?

VIOLENT MAN: I wasn't shouting. No.

[*The POLICEMAN comes in in shirt-sleeves with an
enormous torch. He shines it around until he finds the
VIOLENT MAN then directs the beam into his face.*]

HETTY: Here they come at last.

[*The POLICEMAN walks forward. He is covered in blood.*

He falls to the ground near HETTY. She picks up the torch and shines it illuminating the blood on his shirt, trousers, face and hair.]

HETTY: Did you do this?

VIOLENT MAN: I've never seen him before.

HETTY: He wanted to get you...now look at him. Do you think he's been punished?

VIOLENT MAN: I've never seen –

[*He crawls over to the POLICEMAN.]*

He's alive.

HETTY: Look at him, he's all covered in blood.

VIOLENT MAN: He's still alive.

HETTY: What would we say to him if he woke up. Would we apologise?

VIOLENT MAN: We didn't do it.

HETTY: Somebody did.

[*VIOLENT MAN with two fingers he strokes away strands of bloody hair from the POLICEMAN's forehead.]*

[*HETTY sits down and takes the POLICEMAN up into her arms from behind. The POLICEMAN tips his head back and rests it on HETTY's chest.]*

HETTY: Are you going to run away now?

VIOLENT MAN: Yes.

HETTY: It's sad isn't it.

[*The POLICEMAN is looking at the VIOLENT MAN who looks back into his face.]*

[*The VIOLENT MAN struggles to his feet.]*

HETTY: Do you think an angry crowd got hold of him?

[*VIOLENT MAN nods.*]

[*He looks around for his stick, goes to pick it up. As he bends down and puts his hand on it his arm begins to shake. He puts out his other hand to grab the stick as it jerks around. He falls forward onto his knees trapping the stick with two clenched hands, his fingers caught underneath it, his whole weight pressing it to the ground. He struggles to his feet and walks off slowly.*]

[*HETTY is left holding the POLICEMAN whose eyes remain open.*]

35. 30 Beggars are dispersed

[*The TOWER MAN alone.*]

TOWER MAN: The gates of Highbury swing open. 1000 warriors stream out with feathers stuck in their hair. They need somewhere to go, a drain to spew the poison in their bellies. Thirty beggars crowd the pavement where they want to run: they trample them into the ground and scatter them into the shop doorways...

36. Lost Charm

[*CARROL stands before the SPANISH LOVER.*]

SPANISH LOVER: What's the matter?

[*CARROL doesn't answer but stares at her until he drops his gaze.*]

SPANISH LOVER: Well?

CARROL: Something's wrong.

SPANISH LOVER: Did you come here to tell me that?

CARROL: No.

SPANISH LOVER: You're not so charming any more, I can see that already.

[*CARROL nods.*]

SPANISH LOVER: I don't mean it – it doesn't affect me. You're still a bit childish, that will have to do. You'll probably stay like it forever because it's a fault, they don't go. I'll be here forever, you can keep on coming back, trying again. Sometimes it will be good, sometimes it will be like this. Have you ever worried about me?

CARROL: Worried?

SPANISH LOVER: Yes, worried.

[*CARROL stares at her.*]

About my health.

CARROL: [*Rubs his face with his hands. Holds his hands there a long while.*] Well, there it is. Another visit nearly done with.

SPANISH LOVER: Not quite. Let me touch your cheek.

CARROL: Who's that over by the window?

SPANISH LOVER: That's a friend of mine.

CARROL: [*Walks over to the VIOLENT MAN who is standing by the window.*] What are you doing?

VIOLENT MAN: Waiting for tomorrow morning.

CARROL: How long is it going to be?

VIOLENT MAN: A couple of hours.

CARROL: You've got blood on your fingers.

VIOLENT MAN: Yes.

37. A Message of Peace

[*In the street CARROL and the TOWER MAN.*]

[*The boy is a crowd of people.*]

TOWER MAN: The world is destroyed by war and famine. The bayonet ravishes the belly of the naked child.

I could go on like this for hours.

Would you let a statesman stand at your funeral? I'd rather be a dog.

I will not raise my arm, not even to strike the tyrant. I won't be part of that final struggle. Let the dead bury the dead.

CARROL: Won't you cover the graves of the innocent even out of mercy?

TOWER MAN: I will wrap my mercy in a blanket and search for a place to rest my head.

Why keep yourself alive when cruelty and murder take up all the spare room, from the street corners to the airport terminals, from the empty bowl to the loading bays; the age old secrets of robbery and poison? Why nurse yourself so carefully when they've already given away your allotted time a hundred times over?

38. The Artist Buckles On His Uniform

[*The WRITER and the SECRETARY.*]

[*The SECRETARY is buckling a strap onto the WRITER's new uniform.*]

WRITER: – actually I'm surprised you've stayed with me. I thought your ambitions were only literary. The walls have come tumbling down – I'm going to build a new world and the people that spoiled the old one are going to be punished. Justice! Justice at last. They'll be weeping with regret. Everyone will be weeping. What a spectacle.

[*The SECRETARY pins the appropriate decorations onto his shoulders. The WRITER pulls decorative gloves onto his hands.*]

Oh, if only I could describe how good it feels. Finally! At last! To be on the side that's winning!

[*Pause.*]

Alright, let the day's work begin. Bring in the first witness.

39. A Back Garden Puzzle

[*A cold street somewhere.*]

TOWER MAN: Well, are you fit?

ROLO: Even a lost dog feels fit.

TOWER MAN: How did you lose her?

ROLO: The police came and she fell over.

TOWER MAN: Did you run off and leave her?

ROLO: I thought they could look after her better than I could at that particular time.

TOWER MAN: Listen, what exactly are you worried about?

ROLO: I just can't quite remember what Hetty and I were doing in that man's back garden.

TOWER MAN: He was a friend of yours...

40. Light Shining Out of a Dark Cave

[*CARROL stands before the SPANISH LOVER.*]

SPANISH LOVER: What's the matter?

[*CARROL doesn't answer but stares at her until his gaze drops to the floor.*]

Well? Where have you been?

CARROL: I met a man who looked like you. Do you know what he said? 'Avoid destruction at all costs. Don't even think about it'.

He said he'd seen it all first hand. He said I'd never seen a thing.

SPANISH LOVER: Well, this is a dark cave, you won't find anything here. I expect a dog licking the stones at my graveside. By then there'll be no meat on the bone.

But they're not going to make me do any awful things for them. I won't be part of that final struggle.

41. The Struggle in the Kitchen

[*In the cold street.*]

ROLO: Hetty started arguing and then, oh God, she was screaming and rolling about the place and he went inside the kitchen to fetch a saucepan...

TOWER MAN: What for?

ROLO: To hit her with.

TOWER MAN: Go on.

ROLO: Anyway, she rolled inside after him and, well, those bloody kitchens are so poky, you couldn't avoid, well...she crashed into him and er...well they tumbled over onto the floor and...

TOWER MAN: You went in?

ROLO: No, I was standing in the doorway. Now from what I saw he seemed to hit his head rather badly on a sort of...machine on the floor and...there was a bit of blood. And he...fell asleep.

TOWER MAN: When was this?

42. Immaculate Portraits

[*The WRITER in uniform to his SECRETARY.*]

WRITER: Can you imagine immaculate portraits of every good and kind man hanging behind every window? It will never happen. People will want their freedom. The face they show has deep red lips, she is the very soul of fashion. I once knew a woman who looked like her. She wanted me never to give up until I reached the top.

43. Up a ladder, Down On the Ground

[*The TOWER MAN up a ladder. HETTY is lying on the ground.*]

TOWER MAN: This is no joke. They say I'm courting disaster. They say I'm my own worst enemy climbing up here like this. But it's a habit. I do it for attention. I do it for the good of the audiences. I do it for everyone. What's more I'm scared to come down. Every time I get up here it's more unlikely that I'll be able to come down again.

If I had a whistle I'd blow it. If I had a dog I'd bark, if

I had a wheel I'd burn it. I've had a hundred offers, but I'm not coming down until it's all over. The pavement is burning, the soles of my feet are freezing to my sandals. I'm not a saint but no one can shit on me while I'm up here.

[*He sees HETTY sleeping there.*]

But what about you down there?

Now is not the time to sleep. The spirit is willing but the flesh has been ground down into a pulp. You're not the woman you used to be, I can see that.

[*He steps down to her.*]

What will keep you awake? A history lesson?

44. A Summons from an Immaculate Face

[*CARROL and the SECRETARY outside the circus tent.*]

SECRETARY: You've been chosen to join us. This is your invitation.

CARROL: I don't think I'll come right now. I'm getting on a train in a few minutes.

SECRETARY: There's no need to be like that. Don't you recognise me then?

CARROL: No. Wait. I've seen your face on advertisements I think...

SECRETARY: That's right. Don't you think I'm beautiful?

CARROL: Em...

SECRETARY: It doesn't matter.

CARROL: I'm sorry. I can't really concentrate.

SECRETARY: Don't you ever worry about me?

CARROL: I...

SECRETARY: About my health for example?

CARROL: Look -

SECRETARY: Let me touch your cheek.

[*CARROL lets her.*]

SECRETARY: You're a bit of a disappointment though.

CARROL: I've got to go now, the train's leaving I think.

SECRETARY: Where's your ticket?

CARROL: It's here somewhere.

[*The VIOLENT MAN is there bending down to pick up his stick. His arm begins to shake, he puts down his other hand to grab it as it jerks around, he falls forward onto his knees trapping the stick with two clenched hands, his fingers caught underneath, his whole weight pressing it to the ground. He struggles to his feet and walks off slowly.*]

45. The Story of the Slashing Blades

[*The TOWER MAN and HETTY (supine). He is telling a story.*]

[*TOWER MAN pulls her up and makes her stand.*]

TOWER MAN: The blade doesn't chop once. It goes around and around and decimates the old and the new together.

'...and, and, and, in the dream the great man saw seven fierce birds circling around above him and knelt before his servant and said (shouting above their thunder): [*Kneels.*] "Accept my humility before you. I wonder which of us will get the chop first."

[*She falls.*]

The proud slave's blood watered the sands and nourished the veins of his brothers and sisters for generations to come. A millennium of service humbly appreciated.

By God's Head, woman. Get up!

46. View from the Window

[*The SPANISH LOVER in her dark room.*]

SPANISH LOVER: I used to think you were so special. But when at last I held you in my arms, you were only a little boy. And no more than that.

[*CARROL is by the window looking out.*]

What are you looking at out there? Have you lost sight of it again? Well, you've lost me as well!

Get out of here.

CARROL: Who did I ruin? Whose life did I destroy? My heart is in ruins. The path of true love was a strange one. Was it me did this to you?

I see a man hanging.

47. The Voice of Experience

[*GERONIMO defeated.*]

GERONIMO: Was it me who did the deed?

I don't regret a thing. Better to have tried and failed

than never to have made the effort. I'm not afraid of trying. The lower they make me now the better, it's not my world anymore. I'd rather land on my face in the gutter. Let the dogs lick my bones.

The walls of my mouth cry out.

48. Death of a Philanthropist Fondly Remembered

[*The TOWER MAN and ROLO are looking down at an unidentified corpse.*]

ROLO: I just can't believe that me and Hetty did this.

TOWER MAN: But it seems you did.

ROLO: There's not a breath of life in him!

TOWER MAN: Violence has taken its toll.

ROLO: I don't even recognise him anymore.

TOWER MAN: Was it someone you knew?

ROLO: Yes. He used to invite us to parties in his surgery. Wild parties they were. He let us pay by instalments.

TOWER MAN: He was a philanthropist.

ROLO: He was that. A kind of philanthropist. Now look at the poor fellow.

I suppose he was more like a pawnbroker really.

49. Experience Grants its Blessing

[*GERONIMO, defeated (on all fours), the WRITER in a uniform and trenchcoat stands in the background.*]

GERONIMO: I could have been a great corporate boss

with 45% of the nation's wealth drifting through my fingers.

Or I could have been a judge in the High Courts with the wig of fairness falling down into my eyes. I would have been fulfilled.

Or a merchant banker, controlling destiny like a puppet.

In another life my mother could have been a gypsy and we would have owned nothing, nothing at all, not even the ground we walked on or the ditch they pushed us into. No one could have blamed me for anything.

[*The VIOLENT MAN comes in.*]

Careful! I hold this nation's secrets in my throat. I have a rope around my neck. Just one more tug and it all comes spilling out. I hold the secret of life in the swamp under my fingernails, have the secret of your downfall in my spleen, I have the story of your arrest in my breast pocket. I know what it is to be defeated. You will rise again my friend and you will bear the mark of my cleft stick upon your back. You will say I ruined you. You'll come clean, you'll live in the best of all possible worlds, you'll wear fine socks made out of skin, health care and medical science will be unsurpassed. Take this hand, and I this, and let me kiss the initiation blood on your two fingers.

50. The Willing Spirit

[*The TOWER MAN and HETTY* (supine).]

TOWER MAN: You can't lie there forever. They're repainting the pavements, they're relaying the trees. Don't get in the way when there's hope in the air for Christ's sake!

HETTY: Please I'm tired...

TOWER MAN: He who lives by the roadside dies by the roadside. Come on, get up!

HETTY: I'm drunk, for God's sake...

TOWER MAN: Get up and get out of the way. What's this burning in my eyes?

[*Tears burn his eyes.*]

51. The Hanged Man

[*Outside a building. The WRITER wearing a large coat over his uniform, beside him is a MAN with a service weapon.*]

WRITER: Did you see how he came out in the end? I wish we could show the whole world the picture. After a siege lasting a couple of hours, with all his colleagues either dead or taken prisoner, he finally appears at the door. Do you know what he's got in his arms? To protect himself from the angry gunfire? The five-year-old child of one of his staff. Would you believe it? He holds this kid in front of him and waves a little white handkerchief over his head. As you can imagine, he wouldn't let go of that child until he ws absolutely sure.

MAN WITH GUN: My God. Still it's exactly what you'd expect.

WRITER: After a few years of his job, I shouldn't think there's anything left inside.

MAN WITH GUN: What's going to happen to him now?

WRITER: Oh, we'll have to deal with him on the spot. We can't let this kind of thing get out, it would discredit the service.

We're going to do it right now in fact. Here he comes, stand back. You want to watch?

[*GERONIMO is dragged in and hanged upside down. Out of his clothes fall wads of money and even coins. An angry crowd beat the body with sticks.*]

52. The Martian Spy

[*'Casey Jones'. CARROL is sleeping with his head on a table. ANITA is sweeping up, with a broom supplied by 'Casey Jones', in a lazy good-for-nothing manner. She has the uniform overalls. Her broom clatters against the leg of the table and CARROL is woken up. ANITA sweeps on past.*]

CARROL: I see you've become a member of staff. How did that happen?

ANITA: What? I don't know you, you know. You keep saying you know me but you don't. I don't care what you think. I don't even really work here anyway.

CARROL: Oh yeah?

ANITA: No.

CARROL: I see.

ANITA: I'm a spy.

CARROL: Oh yeah? Who for?

ANITA: The Martians.

CARROL: That sounds like a good job.

ANITA: Yeah. I'm a space traveller. This is the world. I'm in it. So why don't you piss off out of it.

CARROL: Em...[*Shrugs.*]

ANITA: Give me a cigarette. Well, what are you then?

CARROL: What am I? I'm a British Rail passenger.

[*ANITA smokes.*]

CARROL: I went on a train, but the train didn't go anywhere; so I got off and...in fact, it was still in the station so I walked around a bit, met a few friends and what's it to you?

ANITA: Nothing. What if they make me burn you?

CARROL: Why would they do that?

ANITA: That's the punishment.

CARROL: What for?

ANITA: Anything.

CARROL: Sounds just like down here. Anyway, I'm glad you're happy in your new job, because you didn't seem to be doing much before.

ANITA: I was approached for my good looks.

CARROL: It's funny how things change. I mean before today I'd never been anywhere, now I've seen it all.

[*ANITA throws her filter stub on the floor where she has just swept, picks up her broom and sweeps away.*]

53. In the Belly of the Beast

[*Suspended high up in a giant leather bucket: the TOWER MAN, ROLO and HETTY are all down a hole, and it's dark. They are looking up.*]

TOWER MAN: Are we at the bottom of a hole?

Is this the bottom to which there is no top?

Look up. Look up. The sides of this hole are as black as glass. And through them what do we see? The same hole that we are in but upside down.

[*HETTY staggers from wall to wall.*]

TOWER MAN: Can it be that you are the well-known authoress of 'The Pursuit of Happiness'? Is this where your teachings have led us to? [*To ROLO.*] God knows I tried to better myself!

[*ROLO catches HETTY as she lurches past.*]

TOWER MAN: Shsh! I heard the shovels of the sextons burying God. I just pray they don't throw him down here on top of us.

Or was that grinding noise Hetty's teeth? Stop those teeth! This isn't a beauty parlour. The cosmetricians can't help you now! This is a test of our endurance and our worthiness. Pull your stockings up, I can't bear to look.

HETTY: Are you going to let him stand there and insult me?

TOWER MAN: Leave him out of this. He's a far better man than you or I. Kiss me.

HETTY: I'd rather go to hell.

TOWER MAN: I'm sick of all this transvestism. Admit it, you're a woman and I'm a man.

ROLO: Do you think we're safe here?

TOWER MAN: Listen no one cares about your petty crime. It was an accident. Believe me I've witnessed many murders all over the globe and none of them sounded like the one you described. This is the best of all possible worlds.

ROLO: When did that happen?

TOWER MAN: It's been this way for at least two or three days now. The forces of law and order have been torn in two; they're busy gathering their arms together for a new wave.

To tell you the truth it won't be over until we clear her off the freeway.

[*He goes to pick HETTY up off the floor.*]

HETTY: Oh, leave me -

TOWER MAN: Come on, stop complaining. You see the ribs of the giant surrounding us? Well? Are we to be spat out again only to be cruelly struck down by our arrogance?

You marvel at my confidence in such a situation? – I'm just happy to be with friends. [*Starts.*] Who's breathing?

[*They look about them.*]

54. Up in a Hole, Down on the Hill

[*The great leather bucket hole is lowered to the ground and upon alighting the three heroes meet a common acquaintance.*]

TOWER MAN: Hello there, nice to see you again.

ROLO: How do you do.

CARROL: What have you been doing?

TOWER MAN: Finding our forgotten selves, hauling ourselves up by our bootlaces in the old-fashioned style. But we're alright now. How about yourself?

CARROL: I keep hearing foreign tongues. Have we been taken over?

TOWER MAN: No, it's only the inner voices made unfamiliar by under use.

CARROL: There's a sound of rushing water. It feels as if we are very far away from where we used to be. Is this the end of a great adventure?

TOWER MAN: No. It's the beginning. And we're in exactly the same place. Dover – this nation's Calvary.

CARROL: Who's that strapped to the mast?

[*They look at ROLO who is temporarily strapped to the mast.*]

TOWER MAN: It's Rolo. He doesn't trust himself. We are mere characters in his tragedy – he doesn't believe his own innocence.

HETTY: Hello son. Have you got the price of a drink on you? It's this salty air, it gives you a thirst.

CARROL: I don't think you'll find any shops open.

HETTY: Can you not help us at all? Then I think it's best we part our ways here and now.

CARROL: I'm sorry.

TOWER MAN: We forgive you your powerlessness, but I think we all three of us feel overcome by a terrible sense of realism in the face of the long road stretching out before us. We need a few moments solitude amongst ourselves.

CARROL: I understand.

TOWER MAN: We'll meet again.

[*The three stand stiffly, stretched out against the dark afternoon sky laughing and joking together as old friends do.*]

[*CARROL turns around as he sees a figure in the distance; it is the VIOLENT MAN. He is bending down to pick up his stick. His arm begins to shake, he puts out his other hand to grab it as it jerks around, he falls forward onto his knees trapping the stick with two clenched hands and his fingers caught underneath, his whole weight pressing it to the ground.*]

55. Two Strays

[*Epilogue.*]

[*CLANCY and CARROL are talking.*]

CLANCY: So now I walk with my legs slightly apart, like this, like a cripple. What did you think when you saw me coming? You thought I was a cripple didn't you?

CARROL: Yes, I did.

CLANCY: That's what people always think, I can see it on their faces when I approach. Still, I don't care. At least I haven't been robbed for a while. Even muggers think twice before hitting a cripple. I used to wear a wig to try to ward them off, the muggers. I don't bother with that now. I've got this instead. I mean, you just need some kind of defence, and now I've got one, built in.

It's good isn't it?

CARROL: Mmm.

CLANCY: You seem a little preoccupied. Are you thinking about your true love? You are, aren't you? I've seen her. She described you. She's around here somewhere. I borrowed her for a while. I mean I got her to nurse my leg. It began hurting. Do you mind?

CARROL: Em – no.

CLANCY: That's why I started talking to you, I feel a kind of bond.

CARROL: Oh.

CLANCY: You don't mind me saying that?

CARROL: No, I don't.

CLANCY: There are lots of people in the world.

56. The Dance

[*Credit sequence.*]

[*A WOMAN, forty-five-ish, wearing a red dress and a coat and high-heeled shoes with a drink in her hand and blonde hair, dancing to some jazz music. She sways her body slowly in an ecstatic way and has on her face expressions that seem to have been learnt from films or advertising posters. She's enjoying herself floating away very drunk. She's liable to lose her temper if she senses any disapproval. A MAN near her with a cap and a raincoat and an age of fifty stands facing the band shouting 'good luck to you' and waggling his fingers and arm in a confidential way. Otherwise he is still and quiet. The WOMAN, perhaps a friend of his, perhaps not, undulates towards him moving her buttocks to within a hair's breadth of his trousers. She tips her head back with a laugh of enjoyment so deliberate it's almost bitter. He raises his eyebrows, makes a noise in his throat and turns to watch her. He films her with an imaginary camera in his hands, raises his eyebrows a few more times and smiles fruitily.*]

THE END